BORN ILLEGITIMATE

A National Study of the Social and
Educational Effects of Illegitimacy at
Birth and at Seven Years

D1556112

Born Illegitimate
Social and Educational Implications

Eileen Crellin
M L Kellmer Pringle
Patrick West

Published by
National Foundation
for Educational
Research in
England and Wales

Published by the National Foundation for Educational Research
in England and Wales

Registered Office: The Mere, Upton Park, Slough, Bucks, SL1 2DQ
London Office: 79 Wimpole Street, London, W1M 8EA

Book Publishing Division: 2 Jennings Buildings, Thames Avenue,
Windsor, Berks, SL4 1QS

First Published 1971
© National Children's Bureau, 1971

SBN 901225 81 9

Cover design by
PETER GAULD, FSIA

Printed in Great Britain by
John Gardner (Printers) Limited, Hawthorne Road Bootle, Lancs L20 6JX.

703 610

CONTENTS

Contents

LIST OF TABLES AND FIGURES IN THE TEXT

Tables

Figures

Further tables and figures can be found in the appendices.

FOREWORD

THE BUREAU'S beautifully presented study of illegitimacy combines academic analysis with insight, compassion, and a call for positive action. It is particularly welcome because illegitimacy is a subject upon which people tend to hold strong views, often unsubstantiated by valid evidence, and because there are serious gaps in our knowledge about what happens to children born out of wedlock and their mothers. This hampers us in identifying and planning for their needs. Research about illegitimacy is often based on particular geographical areas or on biased samples.

The research team have been able to study a national and really representative sample of over 600 children born out of wedlock. These were born in one week in 1958 and they are compared with all other children born in that week—some 16,000—both at the time of their birth and seven years later. The study provides much valuable information, some of which confirms our supposition, and much of which is quite new.

The findings are a salutary reminder that despite a present tendency to assume that illegitimacy is no longer a stigma or disadvantage to the children concerned, children born out of wedlock are still seriously at risk, both emotionally and socially. In the concluding chapter Dr Pringle makes a plea that we should regard these children, as all our children, as society's investment in the future, and that in allocating public expenditure we should get our priorities right. She sees the poor learning performance of children born out of wedlock in comparison with legitimate and especially with adopted children not as a criticism of mothers who are bringing up their children but as a challenge to society to make use of the preventive measures about which we already know, and to institute a programme of financial and social provision to improve the lot of illegitimate children by making life more tolerable for them and their mothers. It is particularly interesting that with her great knowledge of the needs of all children, the measures suggested by Dr Pringle are in many ways similar to those advocated by organizations such as NCUMC, whose major concern is with this particular social group.

Dr Kellmer Pringle poses a real dilemma. On the one hand, it is necessary for those of us concerned with illegitimacy to know more about the problems of illegitimate children, and to discover whether there is a real 'pathology of illegitimacy'. On the other hand, any isolation of them in our thinking or highlighting of their specific problems may work against their welfare because of society's hostility towards unmarried mothers and their children. They would seem to be best served by 'blurring the edges' between them and other children. Dr Pringle warns us against the danger of singling out any particular handicap and dealing with it by separate services when so many underprivileged and disadvantaged children have similar needs.

This study is of course limited to what happens to illegitimate children compared with other groups of children up to the age of seven. Much may happen to affect and to modify the performance of all these groups, especially during adolescence and young adulthood. It is important that there should be the opportunity for us to know more about the subsequent history of these children, and also to be able to compare the performance and fate of illegitimate children with that of children in other single-parent families.

MARGARET E. BRAMALL
Director, National Council for the Unmarried Mother and her Child
June, 1971

ACKNOWLEDGEMENTS

FIRST OF ALL, we must thank the financial sponsors without whose support this project could not have been undertaken. Sponsorship was a joint venture between three charitable foundations and a government department, namely the Buttle Trust, the Eugenics Society, the Noel Buxton Trust, and the Department of Health and Social Security.

The staffs of the General Register Office in England, Scotland and Wales have given valuable advice and assistance; so did the National Council for the Unmarried Mother and her Child.

Tribute has already been paid in previous reports of the Perinatal Mortality Survey and the National Child Development Study to the generous co-operation of local authority staffs in England, Scotland and Wales, and in particular to the teachers, school medical officers, health visitors and school welfare officers who undertook all the interviewing, testing and examining. Our study clearly depended on all the material they had provided for these two major surveys and hence we would like once again to acknowledge their invaluable help. The parents of the children are also most warmly thanked for their co-operation and support.

Next, we wish to thank our statistical adviser, Tony Round, who was responsible for the analysis and presentation of the statistical material. In addition, many of our colleagues at the National Children's Bureau gave generously of their time at different stages of the project and also commented critically on the draft manuscript; chief among them were Dr Eva Alberman; Professor Neville Butler; Dr Ron Davie; Miss Jane Petzing; and Mr Peter Wedge. The responsibility for seeing the manuscript through the various stages of being retyped rested with Miss Christine Browning and her assistants, and we much appreciate her conscientious and intelligent work. In the arduous task of preparing all the tables and statistical appendices for the printers, we had the able assistance of Miss Teresa Hall.

Valuable suggestions were made by the readers of the final manuscript, Dr I. Blakeney, Mrs M. E. Bramall and Mrs P. Roberts. Last, but not least, we owe a great deal to the understanding and support of our families who put up with long hours of work. In particular, most constructive and unstinting help was given during the final writing up, editing and proof reading of the manuscript by Mr W. L. Hooper, the husband of one of us (M.L.K.P.).

While we are most grateful for all the guidance we have received and for the resulting improvements, the short-comings of this report are, of course, entirely our responsibility.

E.C., M.L.K.P., and P.W.

PART I

FRAMEWORK OF THE STUDY

CHAPTER ONE

Sources of Information and Comparison

Is illegitimacy still a problem?

THERE HAS BEEN a marked increase in the proportion of illegitimate births during recent years. These years too have seen a change in social attitudes towards extra-marital sexual relations. Whether as a cause or as a consequence of these changing attitudes, out-of-wedlock pregnancies occur now with similar frequency across all social classes. Another, and even more recent change, is the fact that more unmarried mothers are now keeping their babies. Yet relatively little is known about how the mothers and their children are faring, either in the short or the long term. Does illegitimacy continue to pose personal and social problems? And if it does, what is their nature?

These questions can only be answered by a careful, and if possible long-term, study which compares the growth and development of legitimate and illegitimate children. If such comparisons can be made on a national scale it is better still since local or regional bias is then avoided. These conditions are by no means easily obtained —hence the dearth of such investigations. However, the opportunity to mount just such a study was provided by a large-scale survey, namely the Perinatal Mortality Survey. Its subjects consisted of a whole week's births and these babies were then studied again at the age of seven years. This follow-up investigation is called the National Child Development Study (1958 Cohort). Each study is briefly described in what follows.

The Perinatal Mortality Survey

In 1958 information was gathered on virtually every baby born in England, Scotland and Wales during the week 3rd to 9th March. This group of children—numbering some 17,000 births in all—is therefore a completely representative cross-section; the term 'cohort' has been coined for such groups and will be used to refer to them as well as the phrase 'the whole birthweek'. The survey, sponsored by the National Birthday Trust Fund, was designed to study the administration of British maternity services and investigate the causes of perinatal death, i.e. still births and deaths in the first week of life (Butler and Bonham, 1963; Butler and Alberman, 1969).

An unparalleled amount of sociological, obstetric and medical information was collected concerning the mother and the course of pregnancy and labour. These data, as well as detailed information on the baby, were amassed at the time of delivery, by the birth attendant, usually a midwife, from ante-natal and labour records, and a record was made of the infant's weight, progress and any illnesses in the first weeks of life. The sociological data were collected in an interview with the mother shortly after birth.

The results of the survey brought into sharp focus the increased perinatal mortality risk which is associated with certain clearly identified ante-natal, social and obstetric conditions. For example, the risk of a perinatal death where a mother was having her fifth or subsequent baby was 50 per cent greater than average. Similarly, increased risk was associated with unskilled occupational status (30 per cent greater than average); maternal age over 40 (100 per cent greater); severe toxaemia in the mother (over 180 per cent greater); and smoking of 10 or more cigarettes daily after the fourth month of pregnancy (35 per cent greater). The identification of these and other high risk groups has led to more concentration of medical resources upon those mothers who are in greatest need.

Our 1958 cohort of children is unique for a number of reasons: it is a representative national group, selected only by date of birth; the very high proportion of returns (an estimated 98 per cent of all babies born in the week) virtually eliminated the possibility of bias; and the comprehensive nature of the perinatal data is at present unrivalled anywhere in the world for a national cohort.

The National Child Development Study (1958 *Cohort*)

In 1965 (and again in 1969) it proved possible to trace and study again the children who as babies had been the survivors of the Perinatal Mortality Survey. This longitudinal, follow-up investigation is called the National Child Development Study (1958 Cohort).

At each follow-up, information on the children is gathered from four main sources: from schools by means of a detailed assessment schedule, completed by head teachers and class teachers; this provides a comprehensive picture of each pupil's attainments, behaviour and adjustment in school as well as information about the school itself and questions such as the contact between school and home. Secondly, each mother, and sometimes the father too, is interviewed by an officer of the local authority, usually a health visitor, to obtain detailed information about the home environment as well as about the child's development and behaviour. Thirdly, the School Health Service undertakes a special medical examination, including measuring height and weight, objective tests and clinical assessments of vision, speech and hearing, investigation of motor co-ordination and laterality, as well as a full clinical examination. Fourthly, the child himself does a number of attainment and other tests.

The major findings of the study of the seven-year-olds have been published (Pringle, Butler and Davie, 1966; Davie, Butler and Goldstein, 1971). The material which was gathered when the children were 11 years old is at present being analysed while plans are under way to re-examine the cohort before the majority of the pupils leave school.

It is intended, provided funds become available, to continue studying the growth and development of the children at least until they have reached adulthood but better still, until they themselves have become parents, because the project provides an unrivalled opportunity to find answers to many important questions which are neither known nor easy to discover by other means. Three of these deserve to be singled out.

First, objective information about normal children at different ages and stages of development is surprisingly lacking; nor is it known how changing social and economic conditions affect this development. By looking at a large representative cross-section of children at various ages it becomes possible to describe their health, physical development and home environment as well as their behaviour and educational attainment. This provides a standard or baseline against which the parent, teacher, doctor or psychologist can judge the development and needs of a particular child; while the policy maker and administrator can judge the effectiveness and adequacy of existing services in the light of the conditions which are revealed.

Secondly, the development of children who have special needs, such as the handicapped or those born illegitimate, can be compared with that of the whole cohort. For example, not only is it possible to establish how many children are physically, mentally, emotionally or socially handicapped but a comparison can be made between their personal, educational and physical development and that of all the other seven-year-olds in our birthweek. One such special study, namely that of illegitimate children, is reported in this book.

Thirdly, the whole cohort as well as the various groups of children with special needs can be examined longitudinally. This makes it possible to study the inter-relationship between social, medical and obstetric factors in the mother, the baby's birth history and ante-natal development on the one hand, and subsequent all round growth and adjustment on the other. For example, a picture can be built up of the long-term relationships between parental social background, low birth weight and the child's level of scholastic achievements. Or how many children, who are backward readers at the age of seven years, are still backward at 11 years; and in what ways they differ from those children who have 'caught up' in the intervening years, or alternatively from those whose performance was average when they were seven and who then became backward by the age of eleven.

In summary, each successive follow-up provides valuable descriptive and normative material about a representative group of British children at a particular age, showing not only their level of development, but also the relationship between various aspects of growth. In addition, and possibly even more valuable, the longitudinal character of the whole project makes it possible to study changes of development in the same children over a period of time.

The study reported in this book provides descriptive material about a national sample of illegitimate children born in 1958; compares their development with that of their peers who were born in the same week as they were; and relates their development, at the age of seven years, to a range of factors linked with their birth history as well as with their mothers' social and personal background.

CHAPTER TWO

Aims, Design and Presentation

General Aims

BASICALLY WE WANTED to find answers to two main questions: who are the illegitimate? and how do they make out? To do so, we looked at what happened, between birth and the age of seven years, to a representative, unselected group of illegitimately born children whose mothers looked after them rather than relinquished them for adoption. Also comparisons were made between the illegitimately born and the legitimate children from the rest of the birth cohort. Some comparisons were made too between these children and those who were brought up by adoptive parents; however, complete and detailed analyses about the latter were not undertaken because a separate study of adopted children is under way. The same applies to children who were received into care at any time during their first seven years of life.

Hitherto answers have not been available on a national scale to the questions which we posed. Among these were: how many such children are there in the population? What is their mothers' social background? What kind of start do they get in life? Are they more often 'at risk', either at the time of birth or subsequently, than those born legitimate? How does their physical, emotional and educational development compare with that of the whole birth cohort? Are there any differences within the illegitimate group between those who stayed with their own mothers and those who were adopted? What is the composition of the household in which they were living at the age of seven years? And so on.

The scene is set in Part I, which also provides a brief review of the most relevant major studies carried out previously. Part II looks at the mothers' circumstances before and during pregnancy, as well as at the conditions which prevailed at birth and during the first month of the child's life; in Part III the children's development at the age of seven years is described and compared with that of their peers. Then in Part IV an overview is given and some suggestions are made for the future.

The design of the investigation

All the interview and assessment schedules, obtained in the two major studies described in the previous chapter, were available for this investigation. Thus it draws largely on data collected, mainly in pre-coded form, at the time of birth and then again at the age of seven years. The mothers had answered questions about their marital status at the time of birth which made it possible to identify the great majority of those born illegitimate in the whole birth week. In the context of our study a child was defined as illegitimate if, at the time of birth, his parents were not married to each other.

We postulated a number of hypotheses which then determined the way the data were organized and analysed. To begin with, some social stigma is still attached to illegitimacy even though this may be changing. In addition, many difficult decisions have to be made or at least faced, during pregnancy, such as whether to conceal the fact altogether from family and friends, whether or not to keep the baby, and so on. Hence one would expect the period of pregnancy to be a stressful time, which in turn may increase the chance of difficulties during pregnancy and the perinatal period. Unsupported mothers are likely to be much more seriously affected than those who are cohabiting; whether or not a woman is or has been married previously might also affect the situation. To enable these suppositions to be examined, the mothers were placed in one of four groups depending on their status at the time of their pregnancy: single unsupported; single cohabiting; married or previously married but now unsupported; and those of that group now cohabiting.

Secondly, in examining birth risks for our sample, one would expect to find a very high concentration of certain factors associated with high perinatal risk for all mothers, in terms of death and low birthweight. For example, having a first baby when aged less than 20 years is likely to apply to a higher proportion of women having an illegitimate child than to women giving birth to legitimate babies.

Higher risks are also associated with lower socio-economic groups. In some previous studies mothers of illegitimate children were found to belong predominantly to such groups, which may account for the long-established fact that the perinatal death rate for illegitimate babies is much in excess of that for babies generally; low birthweight is also a persistent feature in a high proportion of illegitimate babies—a fact which has hitherto remained unexplained. By examining the maternal characteristics of our sample we will explore whether there is a specific 'illegitimacy factor' which ought to be taken into account in the management of pregnancy and delivery.

Thirdly, there is some evidence from our national cohort study and elsewhere that atypical family situations have detrimental effects on children's educational achievement and emotional adjustment (Pringle, Butler and Davie, 1966). A considerable proportion, if not the majority, of our group of illegitimate children would be expected to experience some degree of instability in their family life. Those who were living in a two-parent family by the age of seven years might, however, be likely to enjoy a greater measure of stability; hence one would postulate that they would be showing a more satisfactory level of attainment and adjustment. To explore this hypothesis, the findings for the seven-year-olds in our sample were analysed according to whether they were living in one of the following five types of family situations: both natural parents; natural mother and a step or adoptive father; natural mother and her family; only with the natural mother; with neither parent (either with grandparents or in care).

The sample

Because of the excellent returns for the total birth population in the Perinatal Survey (98 per cent), an estimated 81 per cent of known illegitimate births were identified and interviewed (Table 2.1). This figure compared quite favourably with other large-scale child development studies. For example, Douglas (1948) found that 40 per cent of mothers of illegitimate children escaped interview and Spence (1954) was unable to include 33 per cent of such cases. These results underline the great difficulty of obtaining a complete, representative sample of illegitimate babies and their mothers so that some degree of unknown bias has so far been unavoidable in any national study.

TABLE 2.1: *Marital status of mothers of illegitimate children (other British surveys)*

MARITAL STATUS	PERINATAL MORTALITY SURVEY	LEICESTER[†]	ABERDEEN[‡]	GROP[§]
Single	61% ⎫ 81%	59% ⎫ 96%	67% ⎫ 100%	52% ⎫ 82%
Once-married	19% ⎭	37% ⎭	33% ⎭	30% ⎭
Registrations missing or status not known	19%	4%	0%	17%
Total registrations in study period and area	828	284	699	1,059

†Leicester Survey (1949) reported in WIMPERIS V. (1960). *The Unmarried Mother and her Child*. London: Allen & Unwin.

‡Aberdeen (1961–64) Private communication from D. Gill.

§GRO (1961) reported in *Statistical Review of England and Wales* (1964) part 3, pp. 63–8, HMSO 1967. For figures on which this table is based see Appendix Table A2.1 which gives a breakdown by cohabiting/not cohabiting for these surveys. Percentages have been rounded.

It is nevertheless disappointing that, despite the most careful checking of the records against birth registrations for the week in question, some 19 per cent of the estimated registered illegitimate births remained unaccounted for. Our sample consists of 679 children of whom 12 were twins. The mothers who were single represent 61 per cent of all the illegitimate registrations. This proportion is very similar to that found in other British studies, the results of which suggest that those missing from the survey were mainly women who had been married but now were separated, widowed or divorced; this latter group we shall call 'once-married'; indeed some may well have deliberately concealed the baby's illegitimacy by recording their status as 'married'.

While the great majority of single mothers were not cohabiting, about half of the once-married were. Again this finding is in line with the results of other studies (*Table* A2.1)[1]. Some of the mothers had indicated to their interviewers that they were living in a stable cohabitation. To identify the remainder of this group, we took as the criterion a joint birth registration in which the parents shared the same address.

From the data in the Perinatal Mortality Survey (which recorded the interval between marriage and the first mature birth) it was also possible to identify a group of pre-marital conceptions. Of course, only those whose first child this was could be included, and the interval taken as a criterion was those married at the most for 6 months before the birth. This group constituted some five per cent of the whole cohort. Comparisons will also be made between this group and mothers who gave birth to illegitimate children.

Presentation of the material

Because the subject of this book should be of interest to all concerned with children, it has been written in non-technical language. No specialist knowledge is required by the reader. Tables have been kept to a minimum and the text can, if desired, be followed without reference even to those which are included. All tables have been kept as uncomplicated as possible. The results are usually shown in the form of percentages only, rounded off to the nearest whole number, and levels of statistical significance are shown in the relevant Appendix. There are some further tables in the appendix and there, too, will be found an account of the statistical techniques used, together with reliability figures, levels of significance, and so on.

When differences are mentioned in the text—for example, between

[1]Tables and Figures in italics can be found in Appendix III, p.135.

those born legitimate and illegitimate—it means that these have been appropriately tested and found to be statistically significant. Where such differences are described as tending to be in a certain direction, it means that there was a statistically significant trend in that particular direction.

Lastly, it has been decided not to include all the remaining statistical tables, as has been done in the Bureau's previous publications. The typesetting of such material is very costly and experience has led us to believe that it is mainly other research workers who may wish to make use of it. This will hold down production costs and hence the price. Tables are available, on request from the National Children's Bureau, a charge being made only for packing and postage; a copy is also deposited in the Bureau's library for free consultation.

Definition and relevance of social class

In everyday usage, 'class' tends to have overtones of social prejudice. Frequently it implies also a value judgement, its connotation being influenced by one's view of society in general and one's political persuasion in particular. Used in this way, the term refers to a person's standing—and even 'worth'— in a society which, while becoming egalitarian in some respects, is still organized to a considerable extent on hierarchical lines. Here the term 'social class' is not used in this way but as an entirely neutral description for the occupational group of the children's fathers, mothers or grandfathers, as the case may be.

The classification most frequently used in Britain is that adopted for census purposes by the Registrar-General (1966). Occupational groups are divided into five categories: social class I consists of occupations requiring very high professional qualifications, usually a university degree or its equivalent; social class II includes such occupations as school teachers or managers in industry; social class III is by far the largest single group (containing more than half of the population) and it is usually sub-divided into a non-manual and manual section—in the former being placed such occupations as shop assistant and clerical worker, and in the latter all skilled manual occupations; social class IV consists almost exclusively of semi-skilled; and social class V of unskilled manual occupations.

Thus generally, social class I, II and III non-manual cover 'white collar' jobs and these groups will be described as 'middle class'; whereas the other three groups are almost exclusively of a manual nature and they will be referred to as 'working class'. A summary of these classifications is shown in Table 2.2 together with the proportions of children in the National Child Development Study whose fathers fall into each group.

The reason why social class is used as a yardstick is because it has been shown to be a convenient and useful indirect measure of what might be termed a family's 'style' of life. Hence it embodies a wide variety of environmental influences which affects a child's development; furthermore, it also reflects to some extent the influence of hereditary factors. For example, the fact that children of professional workers are taller and show higher educational achievements than those of unskilled manual workers is likely to be due to the combined effects of 'nature' and 'nurture', rather than to the influence of one or the other alone.

TABLE 2.2: *Classification of occupations*

SOCIAL CLASS	GROUP	NAT. CHILD DEVEL. STUDY
		%
I	Higher professional	5
II	Other professional and technical	14
III⌉	Other non-manual occupations	10⌉
III⌋	Skilled manual	44⌋ 54
IV	Semi-skilled manual	17
V	Unskilled manual	6
	No male head of household	3

CHAPTER THREE

Illegitimacy - Past Findings and Current Attitudes

Some past findings

A DETAILED REVIEW of past studies was presented in a recently published report (Weir, 1970). Therefore we shall give only a brief résumé of past findings except for a rather fuller discussion of follow-up investigations since these are more directly comparable with our own study.

Early research into illegitimacy tended to concentrate on the unmarried mother and in particular on the causes likely to account for her situation. These were thought to be related to her working in menial occupations, coming from a disorganized home background and to being herself psychiatrically disturbed. There is evidence that all these play some part in illegitimacy. However, their importance is likely to have been exaggerated, partly because research had been largely confined to women who sought the help of charitable agencies and most of these women were unmarried mothers. This may well have led to a stereotyped image (Bernstein, 1960; Roberts, 1966). More recently, Illsley and Gill (1968), following the changes in illegitimacy rates in England, Wales and Scotland, presented evidence to suggest that illegitimate births are now more evenly distributed throughout the different sections of society. They depicted a new pattern of illegitimacy, linked with urban living and sophistication.

Studies, based on samples of illegitimate birth registrations in this country, clearly show that the children of unmarried mothers are only a proportion—albeit a major one—of all extra-marital conceptions. For example, of all illegitimate births registered in Aberdeen in 1966, 28 per cent were to married or cohabiting women (Illsley and Gill, 1968). Similarly, the Registrar-General (1964) tried to match the 1961 census returns with illegitimate birth registrations for one month and estimated that of these 29 per cent were to women described on the census form as 'married'; joint registrations, where the father was also enumerated as a member of the household in the census schedules, amounted to 27 per cent of the sample.

An earlier study (Thompson, 1956) identified all women normally resident in Aberdeen who had had an illegitimate birth between 1949 and 1952. Of these, 31 per cent were found to be married, widowed or divorced, and the majority of those having their first illegitimate baby were cohabiting; while of those having a subsequent illegitimate child, a third were living in a stable cohabiting union. In a still earlier investigation in Leicester in 1949 (McDonald, 1956; Wimperis, 1960) some 37 per cent had been once-married and of these 75 per cent were now cohabiting. All these studies show that a proportion of single mothers were also cohabiting.

Clearly, then, mothers of illegitimate children are by no means always single, unsupported girls. Hence in so far as expecting an illegitimate child presents specific problems during pregnancy and at birth, the more pertinent and crucial issue may well be whether the mother-to-be is or is not supported, rather than whether she is married or not.

The trend for both premarital conceptions and illegitimate births over the past 15 years has been analysed in a Scottish study (Weir, 1970). It was found that now 'about one-fifth of all maternities in Scotland are to married women, mostly in the older age groups. Women of between 20 and 24 years old are the most likely to conceive extramaritally, and they have the highest number of illegitimate births. Women aged between 25 and 29 years have the highest illegitimacy rate (per thousand at risk). Teenagers have the lowest illegitimacy rate of all under 40-year-olds, because there are so many unmarried teenagers at risk, and also because so many who conceive extramaritally get married before the birth of the child.' Estimates made for England and Wales suggested a very similar situation.

Noting that there was 'much contradictory information regarding illegitimate maternities . . . largely because of the selective nature of the samples studied', particular care was taken in this investigation to obtain a representative sample of all Edinburgh maternities (Weir, 1970). A systematic sampling procedure by day of delivery was used and the total sample consisted of 288 mothers who gave birth to an illegitimate child between 1st October 1965 and 9th October 1966; of these 242 were interviewed while for the remainder some more or less detailed information was available.

Follow-up Studies of Illegitimate Children

There are considerable difficulties in tracing illegitimately born babies for follow-up studies, partly because of an understandable desire on the part of their parents to remain anonymous; there is, too, a high degree of mobility; these two sets of circumstances may be linked to some extent, while housing and financial difficulties are likely to be further contributory factors. Consequently, the wastage rate is high. For example, in one study of a national birth cohort (Douglas, 1948) 40 per cent of single women were 'lost' within the first eight weeks after the baby's birth. Even when records and contacts are carefully maintained, interviewing such a selected group presents considerable difficulties. It is not surprising therefore, that in this country there has hitherto been no follow-up study on a national scale of the development of illegitimate children after the age of five years.

Two small-scale British studies have investigated the subsequent environmental circumstances of illegitimately born children. Both concentrated on the family situation and on the standards of care as assessed by health visitors. One study covered some 67 illegitimate children in Newcastle (Spence *et al.*, 1954; Miller *et al.*, 1960). By the time they were one year old, the survey had remained in touch with 54 of them. At that time, 27 of the mothers were cohabiting with the child's father, six had married the putative father and one had married another man. Thus the majority of the babies were living with both their natural parents. A further 20 children had been accepted into the mother's family. However, the children's environment was given a low assessment, 32 of the 54 families being considered unstable or in other ways unsatisfactory.

After a further five years had elapsed, the sample was no longer considered to be representative as it had become reduced to 35 children, two of whom had been adopted. Less than half the remainder were considered to be living in a suitable household with a stable atmosphere; eight of the households were described as problem families. The care being given in 'unofficial' families was of a particularly poor standard. Just under half of all the mothers went to work and the great majority of these were living in the home of the child's grandparents. About one quarter of the 32 mothers were working full-time and in most cases had done so from within a few months of giving birth. Only two of the mothers had remained unmarried and both continued to live in their parents' home.

With regard to the children themselves, there was a higher than average incidence of prematurity, a greater chance of death and of being born into and remaining in an unsatisfactory home environment. On the other hand, there was no evidence of a higher rate of infectious or respiratory diseases, nor of enuresis, squints or behaviour problems. It did not prove possible to investigate the extent to which illegitimacy as such had a detrimental effect on the families or on the child's general outlook; nor whether the children were worse off than those from similar socio-economic backgrounds.

The second follow-up study of illegitimately born children was based on some 284 registrations of illegitimate children (for 16% of whom no records were available). Their family situation was investigated five years after their birth when information was available for 238 of them (MacDonald, 1956). An assessment was made by health visitors of the financial and emotional security of the home, and of the physical and mental development of the children. Disregarding the 32 children who had been adopted, it was found that about 70 per cent of the mothers were married or cohabiting by this time.

The majority of children who remained with their mothers were living in quite satisfactory conditions. However, for some five per cent home circumstances were unsettled, creating an emotionally insecure environment which in most cases had had a detrimental effect on the children. Those living with their grandparents seemed to be happy although the health visitors doubted whether their homes were entirely suitable owing to the grandparents' age and the fact that there were rarely any other children present. Overall there were few cases of poor physical or mental development; their severity is difficult to assess in the absence of controls. By the age of five years, some 10 per cent of the children were deprived of both their parents and about half of these were living in foster homes.

One American study must be mentioned here for two reasons. Not only was a first report made recently (Sauber and Corrigan, 1970) but also the age at which the sample was followed up closely resembles that in our project. The subjects were 333 unmarried mothers in New York City who kept their first-born children. They had been interviewed at the time of their confinement in 1962 and were then again interviewed at six-month intervals until the children were 18 months old (Sauber and Rubinstein, 1965). Once more, it was found that 'the task of locating these women in 1968 ... was even greater than had been expected'. Eventually, 62 per cent of the original group were traced and interviewed. By this time the children, now aged six years, had all started school.

A relatively small proportion of mothers were white (only 10 per cent), the majority being either black (66 per cent) or Puerto Rican (24 per cent). To some extent this reflects the fact that white mothers more frequently decide to give up their child for adoption. Most of the women had been very young at the time of their confinement (60 per cent under 20 years) which contrasts markedly with the age of all mothers of first borns in New York City (25 per cent only being under 20).

At the time of follow-up, half of them had married, about half of these to the father of their illegitimate first-born. These marriages appeared to be more durable than those to other men. During the intervening six years, about a third of the mothers had had another child, some 38 per cent had had two or more children and about a third did not have any further offspring.

Compared with the median income of all New York families, the unmarried group of mothers and their children were 'at a very definite economic disadvantage though they did not compare too unfavourably with families of a similar type in the community'. The most disadvantaged group were women who had married but had separated from their husbands by the time the children were six years old.

Perhaps the main conclusion drawn from the study was that 'when we talk about unmarried mothers who keep their children we are not really talking about one homogeneous group but about many different groups'.

These studies described, then, the situation of those illegitimate children and their mothers who could still be traced after a period of years. However, they leave wide open the question of the fate of those lost from view. It could well be that among them there existed a much higher incidence of unsatisfactory home conditions and child development.

Illegitimacy: some current views

Originally, this legally defined status served to protect marriage and all that follows from it, by leaving those born outside wedlock devoid of legal rights in relation to property and inheritance. Some of these legal disadvantages have since been removed. Others remain and function as a social sanction against minority behaviour. The social attitudes surrounding it are likely to die only slowly. Though extra-marital sexual relations have become much more widely accepted, the woman who conceives a child outside marriage still meets with considerable disapproval. It is also still objected by many that to make adequate provision to improve the quality of life for unmarried mothers and their children, is not only to accept but to condone and possibly even to encourage such behaviour.

In consequence, the mother-to-be of an illegitimate baby continues to face formidable difficulties, particularly if she has no other means of financial support than her own earnings and is trying to cope single-handed. Quite apart from the problems and limitations which the birth will impose on her life, a proportion may not want to have a child, or to have it at this particular time and from that particular man. For a shorter or longer time, she may find the whole idea unacceptable and feel unable to face the reactions of her family and friends. While cohabiting women may find it easier to accept the situation, they will nevertheless be aware of the social attitudes towards their condition.

For all these reasons one would expect that carrying an illegitimate baby is likely to be a period of great strain for many women beset by feelings of guilt, shame, ambivalence and confusion. Added to these there may well be doubts and fears about their ability to cope with the practical obstacles, present and future, of building a new life for themselves. For the woman who leaves her home town, social isolation is likely to add to what would in any case be a stressful and unhappy pregnancy.

These circumstances may well affect the way in which the mother-to-be of an illegitimate child cares for herself and her unborn baby; it might also have an adverse effect on the death rate, on complications at birth, and on the chance of perinatal risk. Whether and to what extent this is true, was explored on the basis of the material gathered in the Perinatal Mortality Survey. The findings on this aspect are presented and discussed in the next section.

PART II

BORN ILLEGITIMATE - BORN AT RISK

CHAPTER FOUR
The Mothers' Personal and Social Background

THE SUCCESSFUL outcome of a pregnancy depends not only upon the efficiency of the physiological processes of reproduction but also on the socio-biological characteristics of the mother. In this chapter, we shall consider the mothers' age, marital status, social background and height; making comparisons in every case with the characteristics of the mothers of all the cohort children born legitimate.

Maternal age

It has been shown that, in general, babies of women in the older, as well as in the very young age groups are more at risk at the time of birth. For example, there is an increased risk of perinatal mortality when a mother is over 30, whatever the parity (or birth order), although these tend to rise together, thus increasing the hazards. There is also some increase in pre-term deliveries after the age of 35 years (Butler and Alberman, 1969). Nevertheless, the prevalence of low birthweight babies for the youngest mothers (under 20) and for first-borns, is quite marked.

For this youngest age group there is also a tendency for a raised rate of pre-term deliveries. Among them the mortality rate too is higher than among mothers aged 20—29 years, who are least at risk. This has been mainly ascribed to the hazards connected with a first pregnancy (Butler and Feldstein, 1965), although among mothers less than 18 years old, physical immaturity might prejudice the capacity for safe delivery.

Thanks to the data from the whole cohort, it was possible to compare maternal ages, both for all babies and for first-borns. With regard to the latter, comparisons could also be made between mothers who conceived pre-maritally and those who gave birth to an illegitimate baby. On a continuum of 'stress', the former might be expected to react to pregnancy in a way which results in outcomes somewhere between legitimate and illegitimate births.

Another reason for considering first-borns is that 63 per cent of the illegitimate births were first babies; for those born to unmarried

FIGURE 4.1: *Birth order distribution*

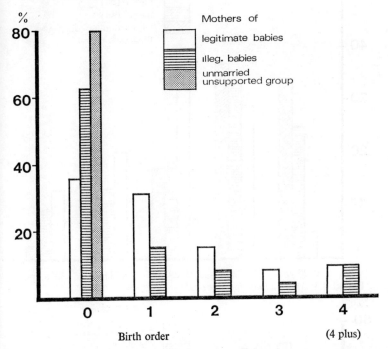

mothers, the proportion was even higher, 80 per cent or four out of every five. On the other hand, among the legitimate sample, only 36 per cent were first-borns (Fig. 4.1).

Clear differences emerge between the mothers' ages. For the legitimate the peak age for childbirth was between 25—29 years; for the illegitimate and the single unsupported mother 20—24 years; and for the premaritally conceived under 20 years of age. Indeed, almost 90 per cent of the babies conceived before marriage were born to girls less than 25 years old, whereas only half the mothers of legitimate first-borns were below that age; this compared with 76 per cent of mothers whose first baby was illegitimate (Figs. 4.2 and 4.3).

The proportion of very young mothers (less than 20 years) is one in every four, or five times as great for illegitimate as legitimate births when all babies, not only first borns, are taken into consideration. One-third of the unmarried, unsupported mothers were teenagers. It is relevant to note that although nearly a quarter of illegitimate children are born to women under 20, approximately

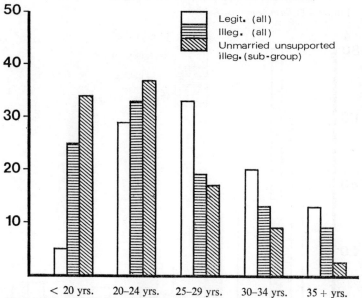

FIGURE 4.2: *Maternal age distribution: all legitimate and illegitimate births (and the sub-group of unmarried unsupported illegitimate.)*

Legit. (all)
Illeg. (all)
Unmarried unsupported illeg. (sub-group)

< 20 yrs. 20–24 yrs. 25–29 yrs. 30–34 yrs. 35 + yrs.

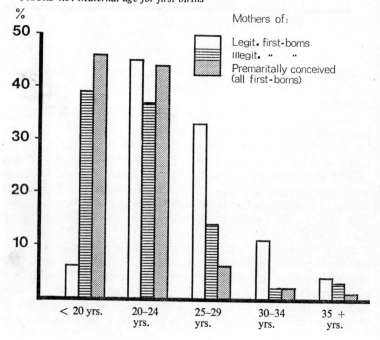

FIGURE 4.3: *Maternal age for first births*

Mothers of:
Legit. first-borns
Illegit. " "
Premaritally conceived (all first-borns)

< 20 yrs. 20–24 yrs. 25–29 yrs. 30–34 yrs. 35 + yrs.

half of all unmarried women fall into this age group (HMSO, 1964). The chances of a 'teenager' giving birth to an illegitimate child are thus smaller than for unmarried women as a whole and, for example, are only a third as high as for women in the 25 to 29-year-old age group.

At the other end of the scale, the proportion of mothers having a first-born at the age of 30 years or later is rather higher for legitimate than illegitimate babies although the pattern is similar (Fig. 4.3).

On the basis of age alone, premaritally conceived and illegitimately born babies must be considered at risk because of the high proportion in the youngest age group; added to this are the risks inherent in first pregnancies.

Regarding marital status, by far the majority were 'unmarried mothers', namely single women who were not cohabiting; the other three groups were much smaller and roughly comparable in size (Table 4.1). The 'once-married' group consists of divorced, separated or widowed women.

TABLE 4.1: *Marital status of mothers of illegitimately born babies*

NOT COHABITING		COHABITING	
Single	*Once-married*	*Single*	*Once-married*
68%	12%	10%	10%

Determining social class

How to assess social class presents a difficulty in any study of unmarried mothers since it is usually assessed in terms of the husband's occupation. Two other possibilities were available to us, namely the mother's own occupation or the social class of her upbringing, i.e. her own father's social class. The former was rejected as unsuitable because we did not know what the mother's usual occupation had been but only what her job was when she became pregnant. Also we wanted to make comparisons with all the mothers in the birth cohort and, of course, many of these would not have been working at all, either before or during their pregnancy. Therefore, the mothers' social class of upbringing was chosen as the social class indicator.

In addition to these practical considerations, there are also good theoretical grounds for this decision. Several studies have shown the important part played in the reproductive process by socio-economic influences of upbringing (Baird, 1952; Butler and Bonham, 1963; Butler and Alberman, 1969; Illsley, 1967). There is evidence, too, of the impact of environmental conditions on childhood growth and adult stature, as well as regarding the relationship of stature to other aspects of health (Tanner, 1960).

There is a further argument in favour of using the mother's father's occupation as an index rather than the mother's own occupation. For many women—and particularly for those who have worked for a relatively short period only—the parental home and its community setting are much more likely to have shaped her values, attitudes and behaviour than the very much shorter time during which she has been influenced by the occupational milieu in which she has been living since starting work.

There is yet another consideration which indicates that her father's social class is a preferable alternative to the mother's own occupation, as a measure of social background. This is the fact that the comparatively restricted range of occupations, readily open to women, tends to force them into a social class band much narrower than that spanned by their social class of upbringing or origin. Thus a relatively small proportion of women born into social class I and II will themselves find work in equivalent occupations, partly because for girls there are only limited openings and in some professions none at all; and partly because long training courses are required for most of such occupations and a much smaller proportion of girls than boys are enabled to take the necessary qualifications. On the other hand, many girls born into social class IV and V become shorthand typists and secretaries, thus moving up into social class III non-manual. Relatively few remain in social class V because here again, opportunities for women are limited.

On marriage, women's social stratification changes once again. This time their social mobility results in a fanning out since it is unlikely that all of them will marry into the social class of the occupation into which they were 'squeezed' or crowded by dis-crimination on sex grounds; a considerable proportion probably move back to the social class of their origin. Hence a woman's occupation is not necessarily, or even frequently, a stepping stone from her social class of origin to that of her husband.

Social class findings

In the Perinatal Mortality Survey socio-economic status was found to exert a profound effect, the incidence of perinatal mortality doub-ling from social class I to V. Despite a changing climate of opinion regarding sexual behaviour, one would still have predicted a difference in social background and upbringing between mothers having respectively a legitimate or illegitimate baby. In fact there is none. It can be seen from Fig. 4.4 that about 20 per cent have fathers

FIGURE 4.4: *Social class distribution of legitimate, pre-marital conceptions and illegitimate samples*

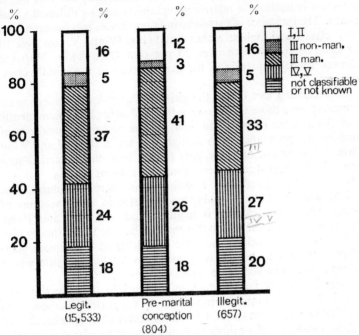

in the white-collar (or middle) class and about a quarter come from families of semi-skilled or un-skilled workers. The proportion of mothers for whom father's occupation was not available or who were otherwise unclassifiable was very similar for the legitimate and illegitimate group (18 per cent and 20 per cent respectively).

Thus our findings confirm that whereas illegitimacy has in the past been associated with low social class, this is no longer the case (Gill, Koplik and Illsley, 1968; Weir, 1970). It must, of course, be borne in mind that this analysis takes no account of the employment difficulties faced by women themselves once they are pregnant and then give birth to their illegitimate child; these difficulties will affect the mothers' own subsequent social class ratings.

That there is in fact 'a striking amount of downward mobility' instead of the rise in occupational level to be expected with increasing age was confirmed in a recent study of unmarried mothers (Weir, 1970).

We also determined within which social class of upbringing pre-marital pregnancies and illegitimacy, were most frequently found; in that analysis, first pregnancies only were looked at. This might give some indication of relative acceptability among different social groups. The incidence of extra-marital pregnancies was lowest within social class I and highest within social class IV and V, just over 10 per cent compared with over 20 per cent (*Fig.* A4.1). Marriage followed more frequently in the manual than in the middle class, however.

An interesting fact is that the girls most at risk of an illegitimate pregnancy were those whose own father had either been permanently away from home or who had died. In this group the incidence of extra-marital pregnancies was as high as in social class IV and V but a lower proportion of these girls (about half only) married subsequently. Further study is needed into the reasons for this.

It has been argued that illegitimacy is more acceptable, less deviant and therefore probably less stressful in those sections of society where its incidence is highest (Rodman, 1963 and 1966). This view is based on a study in the Caribbean. If the theory also holds true in our society, then one would expect illegitimate pregnancy outcomes to be relatively more favourable for girls whose fathers are semi-skilled or unskilled workers.

There is another factor which might work in this direction too. This is that the highest proportion of supported mothers with illegitimate babies was found to be in social class V whereas the highest incidence of unsupported mothers, particularly unmarried ones, was among girls from a middle class home background. Therefore, one would expect their situation to be more stressful in emotional, social and economic terms.

Maternal height

Maternal height has been described as 'an objective indication of levels of health, physique and nutritional status which in turn relate to levels of reproductive efficiency' (Baird, 1952). In the Perinatal Mortality Survey maternal height was found to be associated with both low birthweight and with perinatal death (Butler and Bonham, 1963; Butler and Alberman, 1969); shorter women were shown to be at greater risk (less than 62" as compared with 65" or over). In addition, maternal height correlated with social class, the proportion of shorter women rising with falling social class and lower social class mothers being in turn most at risk perinatally.

No difference in height was found between the mothers of legitimate and illegitimate babies (*Table* A7.4). This is what one would have expected in view of the fact (reported above) that there were no social class differences between the two groups. There was also no difference in height between the legitimate sample and the illegitimate group whose social class category was unknown; this further supports the belief that the missing 20 per cent is unlikely to introduce an undue bias into our results.

Summary

There was one aspect in the mothers' personal background which suggests that premaritally conceived and illegitimately born babies are likely to be at greater risk. This is that the proportion of very young mothers having a first baby was high. With regard to social background and upbringing, no differences were found between mothers having respectively a legitimate or illegitimate baby. Young women, whose own father had either been permanently away from home or who had died, were more at risk of an illegitimate pregnancy.

CHAPTER FIVE

Care During Pregnancy

Beginning at the beginning

THE SUCCESSFUL outcome of a pregnancy is aided by both the quality and the availability of maternity, obstetric and paediatric services. However good and however readily available they may be, they can only come into play if a mother chooses to make use of them and does so at the optimal time. That there has been a general improvement in the maternity services in recent years is beyond question. This is reflected in the general reduction of stillbirth, neonatal death and infant mortality rates.

For illegitimate births, however, the death rate has remained very resistant to change (*Table* A5.1). For example, over a three months period in 1958, the chance of a child's perinatal death for women without a husband was found to be 60 per cent greater than for the whole week's population which was being studied intensively (Butler and Bonham, 1963). Also illegitimate babies are more likely to be born premature and of low birthweight (2,500 grams or less) (Pakter *et al.*, 1961; Sauber and Rubinstein, 1965; Spence *et al.*, 1954; Gill, Koplick and Illsley, 1968).

Therefore we looked at the standard of care achieved during pregnancy by mothers of illegitimate children. To assess this, three indices were used: first, whether the ante-natal clinic was visited and if it was, how early the first visit took place: secondly, the prevalence of anaemia in the mothers as measured by the level of haemoglobin; and thirdly, what arrangements, if any, they made for their confinement.

Ante-Natal Care

If it were not enough to know on common sense grounds that ante-natal care is an important preventive measure, strong supporting evidence is supplied by the Perinatal Mortality Survey: for non-attenders the mortality incidence was five times as high as the national figures. Our study gives clear evidence that a significant proportion of expectant mothers of illegitimate babies did not seek ante-natal care at all and when they did so, it was comparatively late during their pregnancy.

Illegitimate births comprised only four per cent of the week's population studied, yet of all the mothers who had no pre-natal care, half came from the illegitimate sample. This means that the proportion of non-attending mothers in the legitimate group was about a quarter of one per cent compared with 7·5 per cent among the illegitimate group. The difference becomes even greater when comparisons are made only for first-borns. Non-attenders amounted to only 0·1 per cent among legitimate, 0·6 per cent among pre-maritally conceived and 8·5 per cent among illegitimate births.

Early attendance is also crucial. It is only where the mother attends early in pregnancy that the size of the uterus can be accurately related to the period of amenorrhoea (absence of menstruation), so that the duration of pregnancy can be reliably established. This in turn facilitates planning and allows appropriate action should pregnancy complications arise. There are not yet sufficient beds for every mother to have a hospital confinement and hence doctors must make a careful selection of cases who are likely to need it. This is much facilitated by a physical examination at the appropriate stage and by early as well as regular attendance of pregnant mothers at ante-natal clinics. In this way, optimal decisions can be taken about obstetric management.

Again, there was a significant difference between the mothers in the legitimate and illegitimate group. Only 20 per cent of the latter had attended an ante-natal clinic before the 16th week compared with some 50 per cent of the former. Even by the 24th week when the proportion had risen to over 80 per cent among the legitimate it was still only just over 40 per cent among the illegitimate group. (Table 5.1).

TABLE 5.1: *Week of first ante-natal care visit*

WEEK OF 1ST VISIT	ILLEGIT.	LEGIT.	PRE-MARITAL CONCEPTIONS
	%	%	%
No visit	8	·25	1
1—15	20	51	28
16—23	23	32	41
24—31	30	11	22
32—35	8	2	4
36 +	6	·75	1
not known	6	2	3

NB: Notes to this and other important tables can be found in Appendix II.

Within the illegitimate sample, there were some differences according to whether or not the mother was supported (*Table* A5.2).

Cohabiting mothers paid their first ante-natal visit ealier than un-supported mothers (irrespective of whether they were single girls or had previously been married).

Level of Haemoglobin

The older a woman, and the more children she has had, the lower the haemoglobin level tends to be. Since young women predominate in our illegitimate sample and since the proportion of first-borns is high, one would on those grounds expect to find a generally satis-factory haemoglobin level. Not all mothers had their level tested but the proportion who did was very similar for the legitimate and illegitimate, namely about two-thirds of each group of mothers.

The results showed a significant difference between them: some four per cent of the illegitimate as compared with 2·5 per cent of the legitimate sample were found to have a haemoglobin level of under 60 per cent. The perinatal mortality rate was nearly double in the Survey for such mothers compared with those with no anaemia (Butler and Bonham, 1963).

Planning for the Confinement and Actual Place of Delivery

Almost all the mothers-to-be of legitimate babies had made plans for their confinement, numbers being fairly equally divided between hospital and domiciliary bookings. On the other hand, a significant proportion (nine per cent) of mothers expecting illegitimate babies had not made any concrete plans; while among those who had con-ceived pre-maritally some two per cent had not booked. The pro-portion of domiciliary bookings was relatively highest for legitimate pregnancies and relatively lowest for mothers expecting an illegiti-mate baby (Table 5.2).

TABLE 5.2: *Planning for the confinement*

	ILLEGIT.	LEGITIMATE	PRE-MARITAL CONCEPTIONS
	%	%	%
Hospital	49	40	55
Domiciliary	19	42	27
GP unit or private nursing	18	15	14
Unbooked	9	1	2
Not known	5	2	2

In the event, the place of delivery corresponded quite closely to the plans made beforehand. There was, however, a significantly higher rate of hospital emergency admissions among mothers of illegitimate babies who had not been booked for hospital delivery (Table 5.3).

TABLE 5.3: *Place of delivery*

	ILLEGIT.	LEGITIMATE	PRE-MARITAL CONCEPTIONS
	%	%	%
Hospital	50	40	55
Hospital emergency	11	8	8
Domiciliary	19	37	23
GP unit or private nursing	19	12	14
Not known	1	3	0

Summary

Our findings regarding pregnancy management suggest that mothers-to-be of illegitimate babies take less care of themselves; a significant proportion do not seek ante-natal care or seek it later than is advisable, and a significant number make no booking for the confinement itself. Yet it is known that optimal pregnancy outcome relates highly to these various aspects (Butler and Bonham, 1963; Butler and Alberman, 1969).

CHAPTER SIX
Birthweight and Gestation

INFORMATION WAS COLLECTED at birth on many unfavourable obstetric factors, including such conditions as bleeding in pregnancy, foetal distress, abnormal method of delivery, and so on. Whilst the exact relationship of these with the later development of children remains relatively ill-defined, this is not true of the effects of low birthweight. Therefore in this chapter, we focus attention on birthweight—both as a measure of the mothers' reproductive efficiency and as a precursor to the children's subsequent development.

The significance of low birthweight

Not only does a birthweight of 2,500 grams or below greatly increase the risk of stillbirth or neonatal death (Butler and Bonham, 1963) but research can now be said to have established that an above average proportion of those who survive are left with handicaps of various kinds. A summary of research findings in this field, draws attention to the fact that the major part of this impairment has been attributed to very small infants with obvious defects (Dinnage, 1970). There remains, however, a substantial body of recent evidence which suggests that a minor degree of intellectual, emotional and integrative malfunction may be more generally distributed than normal among such children who do not have obvious signs of disability; furthermore, there is evidence that low birthweight leaves a special vulnerability to poor environmental conditions (Douglas and Bloomfield, 1958; Douglas, 1960; Drillien, 1964; Wiener *et al.*, 1965). Physical and mental retardation, poor achievement in school, impaired perceptual-motor ability and speech, and symptoms of maladjustment are among the effects reported.

These findings have recently been confirmed in the cohort of seven-year-olds examined by the National Child Development Study (Davie, Butler and Goldstein, 1971). Being born after an abnormal gestation period as well as having a low birthweight for gestational age, were found to be associated with 'educational backwardness' (ascertained ESN children and those whose teachers thought they should be in special schools); also there was a higher incidence of disabilities of a less serious nature such as clumsiness and poor copying of designs. Additionally, both low birthweight and an abnormal gestational period were associated with poor 'adjustment'. Futhermore, 'handicaps' (severe subnormality and handicaps requiring special schooling) were a feature of the low birthweight group. In the case of the educationally backward children, the effect of adverse circumstances at birth was shown to depend to a large extent on social circumstances.

Maternal characteristics associated with birthweight and gestation

Primiparity, severe pre-eclampsia and smoking in pregnancy were important associations of low birthweight in the whole cohort as was short stature due, in part, to its genetic association (Butler and Alberman, 1969). Maternal age and low social class were related only in so far as they correlated with these other factors.

The indirect effect of a shortened period of gestation on birthweight may itself be associated with three of the above conditions—namely toxaemia, smoking and, to a lesser extent, maternal stature. Also young mothers and those in the lower socio-economic groups contain higher proportions of women giving birth to 'pre-' as well as to 'post-mature' babies.

Findings for the illegitimately born

Because their mothers are younger and because the babies are more often first-borns, one would expect to find an overall excess of low birthweight among illegitimately born children. The fact that their mothers more often smoked and that the incidence of toxaemia was raised (and possibly under-recorded), would reinforce the possibility of finding these results in our sample. From what we already know about the maternal characteristics, the excess of low birthweight is likely to be associated both with a raised incidence of pre-term delivery and with a greater proportion of small-for-dates babies than is the case in the legitimate sample.

Birthweight. The overall picture is, as predicted, unfavourable. Almost twice as many of the illegitimately born babies fall into the low or very low birthweight category (2,500 grams and under) as compared with the legitimate group. At the other end of the scale, there are fewer heavy babies (4,001 grams upwards) among the illegitimate. In fact, the whole birthweight distribution shows a significant shift downwards, with a corresponding difference in mean birthweight amounting to 157 grams (Table 6.1).

TABLE 6.1: *Percentage distribution of birthweight*

BIRTHWEIGHT IN GRAM GROUPS	LEGITIMATE —%	ILLEGITIMATE %
Under 2000	2	4
2001–2500	4	7
Total 2500 or under including estimated	6	11
2501–3000	18	21
3001–3500	36	38
3501–4000	27	20
4000 +	9	5
Total over 2500 including estimated	93	89
No Information	1	—
Mean Birthweight (gm)	3304	3147

Gestation. In general, the mothers of illegitimate babies showed a tendency to go into labour either too early or a little too late (Table 6.2). However, it should be noted that there was no information on the length of gestation for twice as many mothers in the illegitimate, as in the legitimate sample (24 per cent compared with 10 per cent).

TABLE 6.2: *Percentage distribution of length of gestation*

LENGTH OF GESTATION IN WEEKS	LEGITIMATE %	ILLEGITIMATE %	
28–36*	5 *5.4*	8 *9.1*	*2×*
37–38	14 *11.9*	18 *11.2*	
39–41	69 *79.0*	60 *72.6*	
42 +	12 *3.6*	15 *7.1*	*2×*
Not known as per cent of all	10	24	

*Less than 28 weeks were 0.2% of each sample.

Birthweight for gestational age. The illegitimate babies also tended to grow more slowly 'in utero'. Of the illegitimate babies, 12 per cent were among the very smallest 10 per cent of the whole cohort for gestational age (those most at risk as a result of being born small-for-dates). Their mean birthweight even when born at full term did not rise much above 2,500 grams. Higher proportions of illegitimate babies were also found amongst the next lightest 15 per cent of the whole cohort (Table 6.3). A marked discrepancy in mean birthweight between the two samples occurred at each week of gestation in the babies born after the 38th week (Fig. 6.1 page 49).

Analysis of variance on birthweight. On the evidence so far, it could be argued that it is simply the type of woman having an

TABLE 6.3: *Birthweight for gestation*

PERCENTILE GROUPS ON BASIS OF TOTAL SAMPLE	PROPORTION OF ILLEGITIMATE SAMPLE IN EACH PERCENTILE GROUP
	%
under 10th	12
10th–24th	17
25th–50th	26
51st–75th	25
76th–90th	11
over 90th	8

FIGURE 6.1: *Mean birthweight for week of gestation*

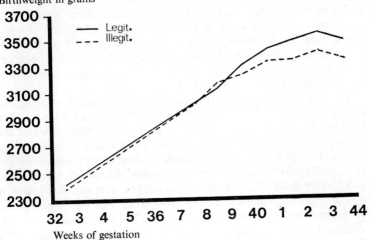

Birthweight in grams

Weeks of gestation

illegitimate child, in terms of the maternal characteristics affecting all births, that explains both phenomena, a persistent excess of low birthweight and the tendency to produce less 'robust' babies in general. This explanation, however, ignores that there are likely to be qualitative differences between a legitimate and an illegitimate pregnancy; and that these may have an effect on the mother's attitudes towards the child she is carrying, as well as on the way in which she accepts and copes with the pregnancy and childbirth.

For the present, illegitimacy continues to be a deviant situation and there are still social sanctions against this type of reproductive behaviour. Not infrequently these facts create tensions and pressures, resulting in a 'stress' situation for the mother-to-be which may well be detrimental to optimal pregnancy conditions in general or which may even be specifically linked to restricted foetal growth. Here we are thinking not only about emotional stress and psychosomatic links; equally important is what the woman does as a result of finding herself in this situation. Overt sanctions may, for example, cause a young girl to leave home; being unsupported, she may have difficulties in finding work or accommodation; being short of money, she may go short of food so that her diet becomes inadequate; prenatal care may also frequently be insufficient—and so on.

These then are some of the likely intervening and interrelated consequences between the notion of illegitimacy as a deviant and still stigmatized form of reproductive behaviour and a physical outcome, such as birthweight. Since we have no information on these aspects, their influence can only be inferred if other factors, associated with low birthweight—be it through the indirect effect of abnormal gestation or the restriction of foetal development *in utero*—are not accounting for differences in birthweight. If, in addition, the outcome is less satisfactory for unsupported not cohabiting mothers (even when other basic factors have been taken into account), this serves to strengthen our hypothesis.

The analysis of variance (presented in diagramatic form, Fig. 6.2 and in full in *Table* A6.1) includes some of the factors known to affect birthweight, together with birth status. It shows which factors are having an independent effect and what their relative importance is.

The effect of birth status (legitimate or illegitimate) was significant in a preliminary analysis; however, when the illegitimate sample was further divided into women who were or were not cohabiting, it was only the illegitimate not-cohabiting group who were significantly at a disadvantage compared with the other two groups. This indicates that when a pregnancy is illegitimate and unsupported, some factor or factors operate on birthweight over and above the other variables. These variables themselves seem to be related to illegitimate pregnancies: the children are often first born, and a greater proportion of their mothers are smokers; toxaemia or other pregnancy complications often go unchecked because the mothers come too late or not at all for ante-natal care.

Summary

More illegitimate than legitimate babies are born with a birthweight lower than 2,500 grams; twice the proportion are of very low birthweight and in general the babies are lighter. Analysis of variance confirmed that it is both the type of woman, in terms of maternal characteristics, and the fact that the pregnancy is an illegitimate, unsupported one, that are important. In the illegitimate sample

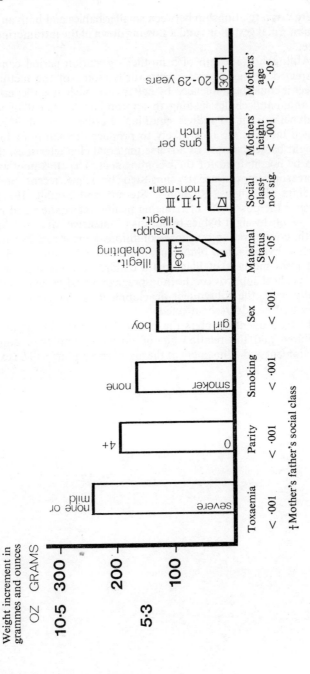

FIGURE 6.2: *Effects on birthweight (analysis of variance)*

Weight increment in grammes and ounces

OZ GRAMS

† Mother's father's social class

there was a relationship between smaller babies and both an increase in abnormal gestations and a slowing down of the intrauterine growth rate.

Although the length of a mother's gestation period can only be corrected in the case of postmaturity, some of the factors which affect it could be influenced by better care, such as earlier attendance at ante-natal clinics leading to appropriate treatment of toxaemia and persuasion to reduce smoking. Furthermore, if it is known which mothers are most likely to produce premature or low birthweight babies because of adverse maternal characteristics, then they can be hospitalized for their confinement. That this may well be of increasing importance is suggested by some recent preliminary findings (Rawlings, Reynolds, Stewart and Strang, 1971). These suggest the possibility of reducing mental retardation and handicap in low birthweight babies by means of intensive care programmes at birth, concentrating on those conditions known to affect the brain, such as hypoxia, low blood sugar and raised bilirubin levels.

Unless mothers of illegitimate children are encouraged to seek the medical supervision, both in pregnancy and labour, that they so badly need, the subsequent development of the surviving children may well be adversely affected.

In subsequent chapters the physical attributes of the illegitimate children and the relationship of birthweight to their educational attainment and adjustment at the age of seven years will be examined.

CHAPTER SEVEN

Mortality

THE PERINATAL MORTALITY SURVEY confirmed previous work, showing that mortality is at a peak around the time of birth and then falls
steeply after the first four weeks of life. How does the pattern of
mortality among the illegitimately born compare with that among
the whole cohort? One might expect the death rate to be higher
because of the higher proportion of very young mothers and of
first-borns; as well as because mothers-to-be of illegitimate babies
were seen to take less care of themselves during pregnancy and to
make less adequate preparation for their confinement.

The total number of deaths, even in a sample as large as that of
the Perinatal Mortality Survey, is too small for detailed analysis;
this applies even more to the relatively very small sample of the
illegitimately born. Under the circumstances all that seems justified
are simple comparisons in the actual mortality rate between legitimate
and illegitimately born children.

Overall mortality up to the age of seven years

The death rate per 1,000 births was higher among the illegitimate
than the legitimate samples (52 against 36); this includes still births
and neo-natal deaths during the first four weeks of life (Table 7.1).

TABLE 7.1: *Mortality, still-births and neo-natal deaths*

OUTCOME AT BIRTH	ILLEGITIMATE	LEGITIMATE	PRE-MARITAL CONCEPTIONS
	%	%	%
Survivors	94·8	96·4	96·4
Stillborn	2·6	2·2	1·7
Neonatal deaths	2·6	1·4	1·9
Deaths/1000 births	52	36	36

Comparing the death rate in the light of the mothers' marital
status at the time of their illegitimate baby's birth, marked differences
were found (Fig. 7.1). The rate was highest among once-married but
unsupported mothers and lowest among single but cohabiting

women. This seemed to be accounted for almost entirely by a much higher rate of stillbirths among the former.

FIGURE 7.1: *Death rates in relation to mothers' marital status (per 1,000 births)*

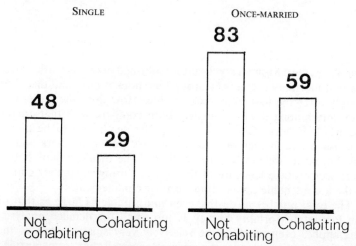

Maternal age, birth order, social class and maternal height

Comparisons were made, for each five-year age group (i.e. aged under 20, 20—24, 25—29, etc.), between incidences of perinatal death among the illegitimate and legitimate samples. For the children of mothers over 30 years old, the incidence was found to be markedly higher among the illegitimate group (*Table* A7.1).

Mortality rates are known to be higher when the mother is a woman under the age of 20 having her first baby. Since the number of such women was higher among the illegitimate, one would expect there to be a higher death rate. However, even when both birth order and age are taken into account, there is still a higher perinatal mortality among illegitimate than legitimately born babies (*Table* A7.2). But the highest rates among the illegitimately born were for the children of mothers having their first, second, fifth or subsequent child.

Among the legitimate sample there was a trend for perinatal mortality to increase the lower the social class but this was not the case for illegitimately born babies (*Table* A7.3). Among them it was highest in social class IV, almost double the rate for the legitimate. However, for illegitimately born babies in the non-manual social classes the rate was also higher by comparison.

Regarding maternal height, the pattern for the illegitimate sample is very similar to that for the legitimate group. The highest mortality rate was among babies of the shortest mothers (under 62″), but in every height group there was an excess rate for the illegitimate sample (*Table* A7.4).

Smoking and toxaemia

In the Perinatal Mortality Survey both these factors were found to have an effect on perinatal death. 'Smokers' were defined as those mothers who reported to have smoked at least one cigarette a day regularly after the 20th week of pregnancy. The risk of death was highest for illegitimate babies whose mothers were smokers. Among illegitimate babies of non-smokers, it was still as high as it was among legitimate babies of mothers who smoked (*Table* A7.6).

Severe toxaemia was also rather more common among mothers in the illegitimate sample; in view of the high proportion of first-borns in this sample, this was to be expected since mothers are more prone to develop toxaemia in their first pregnancy. In fact, the proportion of mothers with toxaemia was the same among the legitimate and illegitimate group of mothers when only first-borns were considered. Yet the actual incidence of toxaemia may well have been higher. Since a higher proportion of mothers-to-be of illegitimate than legitimate babies did not attend for ante-natal care, it is not surprising that twice the proportion of the illegitimate sample had some form of unclassifiable proteinuria or lacked information (*Table* A7.5). The incidence of death was much higher among this last-mentioned group (13 per cent as compared with seven per cent among the legitimate group for whom there was no information available regarding toxaemia).

Birthweight and mortality

Not only was the overall proportion of low birthweight babies higher among the illegitimately born (11 per cent compared with six per cent for the legitimate); but the mortality rate was higher among them too, compared with the legitimate group (*Table* A7.7).

Summary

The mortality rate among illegitimately born babies was found to be higher than that among the whole birth cohort. This remained the case when allowance was made for various factors such as maternal age, social class and height, birth order, smoking and birthweight. It must be borne in mind, however, that numbers were very small and that our findings relate to a period several years ago.

PART III

ILLEGITIMATE SEVEN-YEAR-OLDS COMPARED WITH THEIR PEERS

CHAPTER EIGHT
Home Environment

THE INFORMATION IN this chapter is based on an interview with each mother, carried out by health visitors. The questions were designed for the National Child Development Study (described in Chapter 1) for the prupose of following up the national birth cohort of children at the age of seven years. Because it had not proved possible to maintain contact with the sample during the intervening years, a certain amount of factual information was obtained retrospectively. However, because memory tends to be fallible this was kept to a minimum. Most of the information discussed in this and the following chapters is related to conditions and facts when the children were seven years old.

The sample losses

By the time they were seven years old, some 182 of the 640 surviving illegitimate children had been adopted by people other than their own mothers. This means that of the total estimated national registrations of illegitimate children born in the survey week, less those known to have died perinatally, 23 per cent were adopted. The figure is a little higher than the 20·6 per cent calculated for the quinquennium 1955–9 in the GRO's Generation Study of Illegitimate Children (1965), of adoptions by 'strangers' only.

Of the original sample of 640 illegitimately born children some two per cent had since died, which is twice the proportion of deaths among legitimate children (this will be discussed further in the next chapter). A further two per cent had emigrated and under one per cent—quite a low proportion—had refused to participate in the follow-up study. Additionally, some 10 per cent remained untraced. Finally, there were no data on the home environment for four per cent due to the fact that the health visitor was unable to carry out the interview (*Table* A8.1).

Of the 182 children who were adopted, five emigrated and one had died. Some three per cent of the adoptive parents refused to take part in the follow-up study and some six per cent remained untraced.

Thus the findings in this chapter refer to altogether 504 illegitimate children, of whom 160 were adopted and 344 were living in a number of other family situations. For brevity's sake, we shall refer from now on to the illegitimate children who were adopted as simply 'the adopted sample'; and to the other illegitimately born babies as 'the illegitimate sample' (meaning those not adopted).

The family situation

There was a wide variety of home circumstances among the illegitimately born children by the time they were seven years old. The majority (some 73 per cent) were living in some kind of two-parent family including those who had been adopted. However, only about a quarter of them were with both their natural parents. For the rest who remained with at least one of their natural parents, there were many different patterns: some lived with one or other of the parents, usually their own mother, and a step- or adoptive partner; in other cases, the mother was cohabiting with a man, not the child's father, or living as part of another household, usually that of her own parents or other relatives; another small group of children were with their own mother but there was no stable father figure in the home; and a still smaller proportion lived with neither of the natural parents, being brought up either by grandparents (one or both) or living in a foster or residential home. Of course, during the seven years there are likely to have been one or more changes in the family situation of quite a few children, including one or more different father figures.

As one would expect, a significantly smaller proportion of the illegitmately born sample were living in two-parent families by the age of seven years compared with the legitimate (Table 8.2). This is so even when the adopted children have been added to those where there was a step-parent or some other father figure present in the home. Conversely, among the legitimate a much smaller minority lived either with their mother only, with grandparents or without either of the parents. Almost all the adopted children were living in a two-parent family. The great majority had been placed for adoption before they were six months old (87 per cent).

In the analyses which follow, the family situations in which the illegitimate children were living by the age of seven years will be shown in the six-fold classification set out in Table 8.2; the total number in each category is given in Table 8.2 but in subsequent tables these figures will not be repeated but instead results will be shown in percentage form.

TABLE 8.1: *Family situation of the seven-year-olds*

FAMILY SITUATION	ILLEGITIMATE	LEGITIMATE
	%	%
Both natural parents	27	90
Other 2-parent family (including adoptions)	46	1
Own mother and others	7	1
Own mother only	9	2
Grandparents (one or both)	4	.5
Neither parent (child in care)	3	.5
No data	4	5

TABLE 8.2: *Number of illegitimately born children who live in the different family situations at the age of seven*

Both Natural	TWO PARENTS One Natural Mostly Mother	Adoptive	OWN MOTHER and Others	Only	NEITHER PARENT
146	73	160	38	50	37

The family situation of the seven-year-olds was first looked at in relation to their mothers' marital situation at the time of birth. There were marked differences (Table 8.3). The proportion of children living with both natural parents was very much higher where the mother had been cohabiting when the child was born, whether she had been a single woman or had previously been married; and the last mentioned group were least likely to have had the child adopted.

TABLE 8.3: *Family situation of the seven-year-olds related to mother's marital status at the time of birth*

MOTHER'S MARITAL STATUS AT BIRTH		TWO PARENTS Both Natural	One Natural Mostly Mother	Adoptive	OWN MOTHER and Others	Only	NEITHER PARENT	NO DATA
		%	%	%	%	%	%	%
Un-supported	Single	13	14	32	7	6	6	22
	Once-married	9	6	40	3	12	8	22
Co-habiting	Single Once married	53	—	4	1	3	3	36
		56	7	1	3	9	1	23

The position was reversed in the case of mothers who had been unsupported at the time of birth. A higher proportion had given the child up for adoption and a much smaller proportion of children were living with both natural parents; again this was the case whether the mother had been single at the time of birth or previously been married.

Social Class

It will be recalled that there was no social class difference between the legitimate and illegitimate children at the time of birth, measured in terms of their mothers' social class of upbringing. For the seven-year-olds, social class assessments are based on the occupation either of the father or of the male head of the household.

By that time, there were very considerable social class differences between the illegitimate, the adopted and the legitimate; and these differences are greatest between the first two groups. Almost twice as high a proportion of adopted children (51 per cent) were living in middle class homes (I, II and III non-manual) compared with the population at large (27 per cent); among the illegitimate, only some 11 per cent were doing so. About one in seven of the illegitimate children lived in a home which had no father figure, compared with only two per cent in the other two groups (Table 8.4).

Comparisons were also made between the paternal occupational status of illegitimate children, excluding the adopted, according to the family situation in which they were living. There were no marked or meaningful social class differences between the groups.

Lastly, our study confirms previous findings that mothers from a middle class home background are more likely to give up their baby for adoption.

TABLE 8.4: *Paternal occupational status of the seven-year-olds*

| SOCIAL CLASS | ILLEGITIMATE | | LEGITIMATE |
	Not-Adopted	*Adopted*	
	%	%	%
I & II	6	35	18
III non-manual	5	16	9
III manual	34	30	42
IV	20	13	16
V	8	4	6
No male head of household	14	2	2
Not known	13	1	7

Mothers Going Out to Work

Before the child went to school. The majority of mothers who kept their illegitimate child worked outside the home, either part- or full-time (61 per cent). In contrast, less than a third of mothers of all the cohort children did paid work outside the home before their child was five years old and an even smaller proportion of the adoptive mothers did so—only some 12 per cent. Moreover, full-time work during these early years of the child's life was very much the exception in these two groups, particularly among adoptive mothers. On the other hand, nearly half of all the mothers who kept their illegitimate child were working full-time. Since the majority of mothers had been unsupported at least during some time from the baby's birth onward, these marked differences were to be expected (Table 8.5).

TABLE 8.5: *Mother worked before child went to school*

| | ILLEGITIMATE | | LEGITIMATE |
	Not Adopted	Adoptive Mothers	
	%	%	%
Not worked	39	88	71
Part-time	18	9	21
Full-time	43	3	8
No data	8	12	5

These clear differences are not merely a reflection of social class differences. In the legitimate group the highest proportion of non-working mothers is in the highest social class and decreases with decreasing social class. There is no such decrease among the mothers who looked after their illegitimate children; this suggests that their working outside the home was made necessary in the main by economic pressures, even if reinforced by a desire for company and independence.

This view is also supported by the fact that the number of mothers working full-time was relatively smallest in those families where the child lived with both natural parents.

After the child went to school. Overall, the pattern remained unchanged. Over half the mothers who kept their illegitimate child worked outside the home but the proportion who did so full-time was less than before the child went to school. By now a higher proportion of the mothers of the legitimately born and of the adopted children also worked outside the home, still predominantly on a part-time basis. The difference between the three groups of mothers was, however, still quite marked (Table 8.6).

Looking at this question in relation to the different family situations, the highest proportion of mothers not going out to work was in two parent families. Mothers living with other adults or being responsible single-handed for their child now appeared to have the greatest need to work full-time.

TABLE 8.6: *Mother worked after child went to school*

| | ILLEGITIMATE | | LEGITIMATE |
	Not Adopted	Adoptive Mothers	
	%	%	%
Not worked	42	65	55
Part-time	29	29	35
Full-time	29	6	10
No data	8	8	2

Family Size

This term usually refers to the number of children in a family rather than the total number of people. Here it describes the number of children under the age of 21 years living in a household. The age of 21 years is quite arbitrary but it was chosen because children above this age are likely to be felt, and to exert their influence, as adult household members rather than in the way that younger brothers and sisters do. All children below this age are included, whatever their relationship to each other or to the child being studied.

There are interesting and significant differences in family size between the three groups of children, the illegitimate, the adopted and the legitimate. The proportion of only children is high in both the illegitimate groups: for those who were adopted this amounted to one in every four adoptive families; illegitimate, to one in every five, and for the legitimate sample this dropped to one in every 11 children. The families of adopted children were mostly small, some 82 per cent consisting of one or two children. The highest number of very large families, six or more children, were found among the illegitimate, 12 per cent compared with eight per cent among the legitimate group (Fig. 8.1).

In relation to the family situation of the illegitimate group, the size of families differs in the way one would expect. Large families—of five or more children—were most frequent where both natural parents were living together. On the other hand, in this and the other two-parent group, only children were relatively few in number. Among children living without either parent, the proportion of only ones was high, just over 50 per cent. The two fatherless groups also contained a very considerable number of one child families.

FIGURE 8.1: *Family size in* 1965

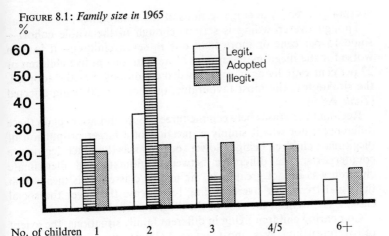

No. of children   1   2   3   4/5   6+
under 21

Moving House

In terms of mobility, illegitimate children (excluding those who were adopted) had had a much more unsettled life than those born legitimate. Half of them had experienced two or more changes of home; and one in five had had four or more moves, compared with one in 14 among the sample as a whole.

Comparing mobility in relation to the different family situations, mothers living in another household had made the fewest moves. Rather unexpectedly, children living with their mother only, had also had relatively few moves although in three cases there were more than ten moves in the first seven years of the child's life. The most unsettled were two-parent families; this was particularly so where one was the child's natural parent, some 38 per cent having had four or more moves within the child's first seven years of life.

Overcrowding

The definition used here is that adopted by the Registrar-General for the 1961 census. Overcrowding is assessed by the total number of persons in a household, irrespective of age or sex, divided by the number of living rooms and bedrooms in the house. For this purpose the kitchen is counted as a room if it is used for eating or sleeping. According to this definition, a child is considered to be in over-crowded conditions if he is living in a household with more than 1·5 people per room. This is by no means a luxurious standard. Indeed, the Milner Holland report 'Housing in Greater London' (HMSO, 1965) considered it to lag 'far behind what is regarded as acceptable even by average sections of the community'.

Though overcrowding is serious enough in the whole cohort—some 15 per cent or more than one in seven children—it is even worse for the illegitimate sample. More than one in five children or 22 per cent were living in overcrowded conditions. For the adopted, the situation is the most favourable, only one in 20 being affected (*Table* A8.9).

Regional variations between the three groups did not explain these differences; nor was it simply a question of a larger proportion of illegitimate children being in lower social classes than their legitimate counterparts. The difference between legitimate and illegitimate children was in fact greatest in the middle classes. This means that the usual trend, for overcrowding to increase the lower the social class, was absent in the case of the illegitimately born.

Comparing children living in different family situations, the extent of overcrowding was most severe—almost one in every three children—among those living with both their natural parents. This is not unexpected since this is the group in which there was the highest proportion of large families. In the other groups, the extent of overcrowding was roughly similar to that found in the cohort as a whole.

Household Amenities

Space allows some degree of privacy and room to play, but the physical quality of the home environment also depends on the availability of basic amenities. Hence we inquired whether the family had the sole or shared use of the following: an indoor lavatory, hot water supply, a bathroom and cooking facilities.

In this respect, too, illegitimate children were very much worse off than the legitimate or the adopted. Some 33 per cent—one in three—lived in a home which lacked the sole or shared use of one or more of these basic amenities. The comparable incidence for the other two groups is 17 per cent and five per cent respectively. Similarly, the proportion of illegitimate children whose home had only one of these basic amenities, on a shared or sole use basis, is three times as high as for the legitimate whereas among the adopted the number was a mere one per cent.

Looking at each of these amenities in turn, among the illegitimate one in every five homes lacked the comfort of hot water supply, a similar proportion had no bathroom and over a quarter did not have an indoor lavatory; some five per cent of their mothers had even to share cooking facilities. Among the legitimate sample the incidence was half or less this proportion.

In one respect only are the illegitimate on an equal footing with the other two groups of children, namely in the use of a garden or yard in which to play.

In the whole cohort there was a marked social class effect, children in social class V households being 12 times more likely to lack or to have to share three of the basic amenities than those in middle-class homes. This difference was much less marked for the illegitimate group, social class V families being twice as likely as middle class ones to lack or to have to share amenities. In fact, there was no significant social class trend. Nor were there any marked differences in the availability of the basic amenities between the different family situations in which the illegitimate children were living.

Housing, Financial and Employment Problems

No specific questions were asked to elicit the presence of any of these problems but health visititors simply noted them where they were overtly in evidence. Hence it is likely that their incidence is underestimated, since such problems are not always obvious and felt anxieties may not be apparent.

Three of the major problems were analysed for this study, namely problems of housing, finance and employment or lack of it. All were two to three times more frequent among the illegitimate than the legitimate; among the adopted group they hardly featured at all (*Table* A8.13).

When these problems were analysed in relation to different family situations, they were of course present in all the different groups but there were no very marked differences in incidence with one exception. This was the group of mothers who were on their own without a father figure or other family support: among them there was a much higher proportion suffering from financial hardship (some 43 per cent) than in any other group.

Use of Day and Residential Care Facilities

Since nearly half of the mothers of illegitimate children worked full-time before the child went to school, one would expect a considerable proportion to require day care facilities of one kind or another. We have information only about day nurseries, run privately or by local authorities. A much higher proportion of illegitimate than legitimate children attended such nurseries (20 per cent as against six per cent).

Because of the multiplicity of problems—finance, housing and employment—which beset the families of illegitimate children one would also predict that a considerable number would have to be taken 'into care' for longer or shorter periods. This was the case, 38 children, or one in nine, having had separation experiences of this kind, compared with one in 50 in the whole cohort. Of these 38 children, six had been in care for almost their entire life. Overall, they had experienced 77 receptions into care which means that those children who came into care did so on average twice by the time they were seven years old. In half the cases the first separation from their home and parents occurred before they were 18 months old and for a quarter this happened within their first five months of life. At the time of reception into care, 90 per cent were under the age of five years—the very years when children are believed to be most vulnerable to the ill-effects of separation from their parents.

Some evidence was also available on the reasons which precipitated reception into care. In the case of unsupported mothers difficulties in finding accommodation was the most frequent single reason accounting for half the cases; next came her being taken ill; while for the remainder, mental illness, a second confinement and her desertion of the baby made the child's removal necessary. Among supported mothers the preponderant reasons were confinement and some physical illness, together accounting for about half the cases; next came housing problems and then desertion of the baby.

Among the adopted sample, the proportion of children being received into care was even higher than among the illegitimate, but in their case this is due indirectly to their becoming available for adoption: in many such cases a child spends a period of time in substitute care until a suitable adoptive home has been found and all the necessary formalities have been completed.

In relation to the different family situations, children living with both their natural parents had the least need, and hence the lowest incidence, of using day or residential care facilities. However, even so, the proportion was markedly higher than among the legitimate. The highest need for substitute care was found among children who remained with their own mothers but where there was no father figure or other supporting relatives. The extremely high incidence of children who have experienced long-term residential care among those without either parent, is a reflection of the fact that a high proportion of them have been deprived of normal family life for a major part of their lives.

Summary

In all aspects which were examined the home environment of the illegitimately born children was more unfavourable than that of the legitimate or of those, also illegitimate, who were subsequently adopted. Indeed, the last mentioned group grew up under the most favoured conditions. In contrast, there had been a marked degree of downward social mobility among the families who had not given up the illegitimate child for adoption.

A high proportion among the illegitimate sample lived in a home which had no father figure; a majority of the mothers went out to work, both before and after the child went to school; mobility was high and so was the degree of overcrowding; a third of the children's homes lacked the use of one or more of such amenities as an indoor lavatory, hot water supply, a bathroom and their own cooking facilities; and a high proportion of the children experienced some form of substitute care, either on a day or residential basis.

CHAPTER NINE
Physical Development

THE INFORMATION in this chapter is based partly on the health visitor's interview with the mother, partly on the special medical examination carried out for the study and partly on answers supplied by the children's teachers. Comparisons will be made between the legitimate, the illegitimate and the adopted children, and where there is a possible link between subsequent physical development and events at birth, the total group of illegitimately born children is combined for comparison with the legitimate sample.

Deaths before the age of seven years

A significantly greater number of illegitimate children died during the first seven years of life than did among the legitimate. Of those who were not relinquished for adoption, four babies died before their first birthday; three of them from broncho-pneumonia, one of whom also suffered from gastro-enteritis and debility; for the fourth the cause of death is unknown but his birthweight had been very low.

The proportion of children who died from accidents was also higher among the illegitimate than the legitimate. One was a cot accident at the age of one year; two children died when five years of age, one by drowning and the other as a result of an accident on a building site. Two children died as toddlers, one from encephalitis and the other from febrile convulsions. Another, who died at four and a half years, had a congenital abnormality, and the 11th death was from carcinomatosis (Wilm's tumour) at the age of one year. Only one of the adopted children had died and this was the result of a landslip.

A later inquiry, covering the period 1964–66, similarly found a much higher post-neonatal death rate for illegitimate than for legitimate infants (Riley, 1970). In addition to the general indications that prematurity obviously has continuing significance into the post-natal period the author concludes that 'assuming some other underlying factor is not really responsible for the difference, illegitimacy must be considered a risk factor'.

Proportion of boys and girls
At the age of seven years the sexes were equally balanced among the legitimate sample. In contrast, there was a lower proportion of girls among the illegitimate who had been adopted and a higher proportion among those not adopted, which means that more mothers kept girls than boys (*Table* A9.4).

Prevalence of physical defects
There is no indication that difficult perinatal conditions have led to an increased incidence of physical defects among all the illegitimately born by the time they were seven years old. For example, in the whole cohort, the proportion of children who had been formally ascertained as in need of special education (some 1·3 per cent) agreed well with national statistics (DES, 1969). Among the illegitimate, the figure was even less (0·6 per cent); two children, designated 'educationally subnormal', were living with both their natural parents and a third, partially sighted child, had been eventually adopted. Initially, he had been fostered privately until the mother became unable to keep up the required payments. After being taken into care, he was then placed in a foster home but this placement did not work out. So he was moved again to another foster home and by the time he was four years old these foster parents decided to adopt him.

Similarly, with regard to congenital heart disease, heart murmurs, asthma and fits, the proportion reported among the illegitimate was the same, or lower, than for the whole cohort. The congenital abnormalities consisted of two cases of congenital heart disease, one child with a hare lip and one with some minor deformity of the ribs.

Accidents requiring hospital admission
Apart from the disproportionately high number of deaths from accidents among the illegitimate (reported above), the proportion of children admitted to hospital as a result of at least one accident was very similar among the illegitimate sample, those who had been adopted and the legitimate children (*Table* A9.2.) Relatively speaking, the most accident-prone group seemed to be children living with their own mother without any support from a father figure or family, one in three such children needing to go to hospital. This might be due to a higher proportion having to be with child minders, some of whom are known to be unsatisfactory; or it may be that such children have to learn to fend for themselves earlier and hence are more likely to be exposed to hazardous situations; some psycho-

logical factors may also be involved; or maybe a combination of all these factors plays a part. No light can be shed on this question by our study but the problem merits further investigation.

Growth, vision, hearing, speech intelligibility and co-ordination

Teachers were asked to say how each child compared for height and weight with his class mates. No differences were found between the legitimate and the illegitimate who had not been adopted, but there tended to be more tall children among the adopted compared with the rest of the illegitimate group. The proportion of very light children was similar in all three groups whereas there were relatively fewer very heavy children among both groups of the illegitimate.

The evidence on the age by which the children were able to walk and talk, is based on questions put to mothers by health visitors. As it was obtained restrospectively, the possibility of some bias due to faulty memory cannot be ruled out. In the event, there was virtually no difference between the illegitimate, the adopted and the legitimate samples in the proportion of children who were reported to be late in either walking or talking (i.e. not able to do so by 18 and 24 months respectively).

The same results were obtained for vision as well as hearing. School medical officers administered special tests and also made a detailed clinical assessment of every child in the whole cohort. There was no difference in the prevalence of sensory impairment between all the illegitimately born children and the legitimate sample.

The medical examiners were also asked to assess the overall intelligibility of each child's speech on a four-point scale. Again, there was no difference between all illegitimate and legitimately born children but the illegitimate not-adopted group contained more children whose speech was not clearly intelligible by comparison with the legitimate. However, since poor speech was found to be associated with lower social class in the main study (Davie *et al.*, 1971), it is likely that this is also the reason for this finding.

Two further aspects related to physical development were analysed, namely poor co-ordination and restlessness. Both are to some extent linked to maturation, since with increasing age co-ordination improves and periods of concentration lengthen. At the same time it is still an open question to what extent clumsiness and being fidgety are due to environmental and emotional influences. Minor neurological impairment may also be associated with either condition.

Teachers were asked whether or not a child was clumsy, had poor physical co-ordination or showed fidgety, restless behaviour. A higher proportion of these difficulties was found among the illegiti-

mately born, whether or not they had been adopted, than among
the legitimate children (Tables 9.1 and 9.2).

TABLE 9.1: *Teacher's assessment of clumsiness*

RATING	LEGITIMATE	ALL ILLEGITIMATE
	%	%
Not at all	87	82
Somewhat	11	14
Certainly	2	4

TABLE 9.2: *Teacher's assessment of restless behaviour*

RATING	LEGITIMATE	ALL ILLEGITIMATE
	%	%
Not at all	76	70
Somewhat	17	19
Certainly	7	11

Attendance at infant welfare clinics

The use mothers make of child health clinics during the first
year of a baby's life is just one indication of the standard of maternal
care. A comparison between the three groups shows that two out of
every three of the adopted were regularly taken to a local authority
welfare clinic whereas this was the case for less than half of the
illegitimate non-adopted group. Conversely, the proportion of
children who did not attend at all was twice as large in the latter
group. The attendance figures for the legitimate sample fell in
between the other groups, so that once again, the most favoured
were those who had been adopted (Table 9.3).

TABLE 9.3: *Attendance at infant welfare clinic up to the age of 1 year*

ATTENDANCE	ILLEGITIMATE Not Adopted	Adopted	LEGITIMATE
	%	%	%
Regular	42	66	57
Occasional	24	11	20
Not attended	31	15	22
Not known	3	8	1

Summary

The proportion of children who died during the first seven years
of life was greater among the illegitimate than the legitimate group.
However, there was no difference in the prevalence of physical

defects between all the illegitimate and the legitimate. With regard to physical growth, the achievement of such developmental milestones as walking and talking, and admission to hospital for accidents the illegitimate not-adopted child did as well as the legitimate and the adopted, although the latter had a higher proportion of tall children than either of other two groups. On vision, hearing and intelligibility of speech there were no differences between all the illegitimately born and the rest; however, illegitimate children who were not adopted had a higher proportion with poor speech at the age of seven years than either of the other two groups.

In two respects both illegitimate groups, the adopted and the not-adopted, showed a higher incidence of difficulties, namely there were more clumsy and restless children among them. Lastly, fewer mothers of the illegitimate children paid regular visits to child health clinics during the baby's first year of life than did the adoptive mothers or those of the whole cohort; and a significantly higher proportion never went at all.

CHAPTER TEN

Ability and Attainment

THE TEACHERS of all the children in the cohort completed an educational assessment booklet. This provided information about the relationship between the school and the parents as well as about assessments made by the teacher of each pupil's abilities and attainments. Also the child himself was given four tests to measure directly a number of different abilities.

First, to obtain an indication of the children's general mental and perceptual development as well as of other maturational aspects, the 'Draw-a-man' test was given (Harris, 1963). Secondly, to assess perceptual-motor ability, the 'Copying designs' test was administered. This consists of six designs—a circle, square, triangle, diamond, cross and star—each of which the child is asked to copy twice. However, time precluded the analysis of this test.

Thirdly, the Southgate Test (1962) was used to obtain an objective assessment of reading ability. Basically this measures word recognition skills. In the first and easier part, the child selects from a number of words the one which corresponds to a picture in the test booklet; for later items, the teacher reads out a word which the child has to identify from among a number of other words in front of him.

The fourth is a problem arithmetic test, which consists of ten problems, graded in level of difficulty. Teachers were asked to read the problems to poor readers so as to avoid penalizing their performance on this test because of their reading backwardness.

The ability and attainment of the children will be considered also in relation to some of the important factors, known to affect attainment and performance, such as social class, family size, the child's sex, changes of school and parental interest in their children's education. The relative effects of birthweight will also be taken into account.

Level of general knowledge
Teachers were asked to rate each child on a five point scale. The descriptions provided ranged from 'exceptionally well-informed for

his age' to 'largely ignorant of the world around him'. A child's level of general knowledge is to a large extent influenced by the opportunities and stimulation provided for him by his family. This was clearly shown in the results obtained for the whole birth cohort where only some 10 per cent of middle class children were below average compared with about 40 per cent in the manual social classes.

FIGURE 10.1: *Proportion of children with 'below average' general knowledge: teachers' ratings (per cent)*

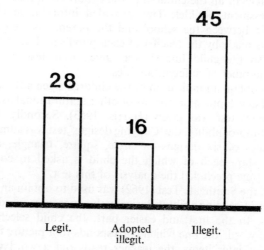

The ratings obtained respectively by the illegitimate, adopted and legitimate samples showed marked differences. About one in three children among the adopted and one in four among the legitimate were considered by their teachers to be above average in general knowledge compared with only one in ten of the illegitimate (i.e. 35 per cent, 23 per cent and 10 per cent). Conversely, almost half of the illegitimate group were judged to be below average in this respect compared with about a quarter and one in six among the legitimate and adopted children respectively (Fig. 10.1). Similar differences were found between boys and girls in each of the groups.

Since there were differences in social class composition between the three groups (Chapter 8), we explored whether these accounted for the differences found in general knowledge level. This is not the case. On the contrary, the generally unfavourable background of the illegitimate sample appeared to have a detrimental effect even on children living in middle class homes; thus only some 24 per cent from such homes were rated as above average in general knowledge, compared with some 41 per cent among the legitimate sample from homes in the non-manual social classes. On the other hand, there was not such a marked differential effect from growing up in a manual social class home: among the legitimate and illegitimate sample, the proportion rated above average from such homes was 15 per cent and 10 per cent respectively.

Opposite effects obtained for the adopted sample. Among those living in manual class homes, twice as many were rated above average as among the legitimate children from the same social class background (29 per cent as against 15 per cent). On the other hand, about the same proportion of adopted and legitimate children were rated above average in middle class homes 43 per cent as against 41 per cent). Thus it seems that the generally favourable environment of adoptive homes counteracts to some extent even unfavourable social class effects; while for the illegitimate even favourable social class effects are partly reduced by their generally more unfavourable home backgrounds.

Level of oral ability

Again, this was rated by teachers on a five-point scale. The descriptions provided ranged from 'expresses himself well in conversation' to 'markedly poor oral ability'. Power of self-expression relates, of course, to the level of conversation and verbal stimulation generally in a child's home. Hence there is a close link between this ability and social class. For the whole birth cohort this was shown by the fact that among middle class children only some eight per cent scored below average as against about 31 per cent in the manual social classes.

The differences between the illegitimate, the adopted and the legitimate were marked and of a similar order as those for general knowledge (Fig. 10.2). The last mentioned occupied a middle position and the adopted once again achieved the highest proportion of favourable and the lowest proportion of unfavourable ratings while the illegitimate did worst (favourable respectively 38 per cent, 26 per cent and 16 per cent: unfavourable respectively 14 per cent, 21 per cent and 32 per cent). Similar differences were also found when boys and girls were considered separately.

With regard to the relative effects of social class, even within the favourable middle class social background the proportion of illegitimate children above average in oral ability was still lower than among the legitimate middle class children (27 per cent as against 42 per cent). On the other hand, there was not a differential effect from growing up in a manual social class home; the proportion rated above average was very similar among the legitimate and illegitimate samples (nine per cent and 11 per cent respectively).

TABLE 10.2: *Proportion of children with 'below average' oral ability: teachers' ratings (per cent)*

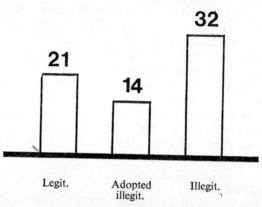

Overall the adopted sample did not differ much from the legitimate group in the proportion of children rated either above average (46 per cent and 42 per cent) or below average (14 per cent and nine per cent) in oral ability. Once again, however, adopted children in working class homes received higher ratings than the legitimate from the same social background.

Level of creativity

To help define this concept in as wide a context as possible, it was suggested to teachers that it should be judged in relation to the whole range of creative activities, including free writing, story telling, handwork, painting and dramatic work. The five-point scale provided for the ratings used the following descriptions at the top and bottom end: 'shows marked originality or creativity in most areas'; and 'never shows a trace of originality or creativity in any of his work'.

One would expect this characteristic to be relatively less affected by a child's home background than those considered previously. The findings for the whole birth cohort confirm this supposition, since among middle class children about 18 per cent scored below average compared with 40 per cent in the manual social classes.

A significantly smaller proportion of the illegitimate were rated above average compared with the legitimate and the adopted groups whose proportions were practically identical (both 20 per cent as against 13 per cent); the position was similar regarding the proportions who were said to lack creativity, namely one in three children among the legitimate and the adopted, and almost one in two among the illegitimate (Fig. 10.3). There were similar differences for boys and girls separately.

FIGURE 10.3: *Proportion of children 'below average' in 'creativity': teachers' ratings (per cent)*

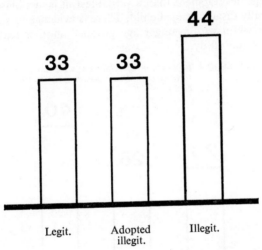

With regard to social class effects, the more favourable middle class background did not exert a marked differential influence on the three groups as far as above average creativity is concerned (28 per cent were so rated among the legitimate and among the adopted and 22 per cent among the illegitimate); however, the highest proportion of children from middle class homes rated below average was in the adopted group so that the order was reversed for once in relation to the illegitimate (respectively 35 per cent adopted, 24 per cent illegitimate, and 18 per cent legitimate).

Similarly, differences were comparatively small in the proportions rated below or above average in each of the three groups, when children from manual class homes were considered (above average: legitimate 15 per cent; adopted 19 per cent; illegitimate 14 per cent; below average: legitimate 40 per cent; adopted 32 per cent; illegitimate 47 per cent). Nevertheless, the tendency for adopted children to do best remains, and this was particularly marked in the semi-skilled and unskilled social groups.

Draw-a-man test

There is no very satisfactory group intelligence test for seven-year-olds, particularly for those who are less able, yet the only really reliable alternative, namely giving an individually administered test, was not a practical possibility. Nor can the Draw-a-man test be considered a valid substitute for an individual test (Pringle, 1963). However, it does provide some indication of a child's maturing intellect and perceptual development; moreover, being less dependent on language development than a verbal test, it is less biased against the culturally disadvantaged child. There is evidence to suggest that it is more useful with younger age groups—another reason for its inclusion in this study.

FIGURE 10.4: *Proportion of children with poor performance on Draw-a-man test:* (0–19) (*per cent*)

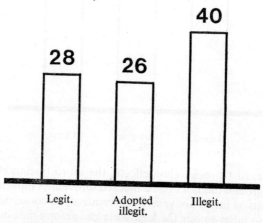

Once again, the performance of the illegitimate group was clearly the worst. None received a top score in contrast to the legitimate and the adopted (one per cent and six per cent did); and conversely, some three per cent of the illegitimate received scores in the bottom group while none of the adopted and only one per cent of the legitimate did so. When scoring below average is taken as the criterion the proportion was again much higher among the illegitimate than the legitimate or the adopted (Fig. 10.4).

Reading attainment

This was assessed by two means, an objective test and the teacher's rating of each child's achievement on a five-point scale. The descriptions of the five categories ranged from 'avid reader, reads fluently and widely for his age' to 'non-reader, or recognizes a few words only'.

The results of the (Southgate) reading test show the adopted to have the highest proportion and the illegitmate the lowest proportion of good readers. The contrast was even more marked regarding poor readers: one of every two of the illegitimate children did very badly in this subject, compared with fewer than one in three among the whole cohort and fewer than one in every six among the adopted (Fig. 10.5). A very similar picture emerges from the teachers' ratings.

FIGURE 10.5: *Proportion of children with poor reading ability: (Southgate test 0–20) (per cent)*

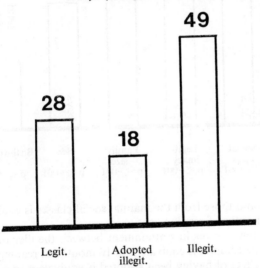

Then the combined effects on reading of the following factors were examined: social class; legitimacy status (i.e. illegitimate, adopted or legitimate); family size (i.e. the number of children in the household when the child was seven years old); the child's sex; and his birth-weight. The results are shown in terms of the gain in months of reading age (Fig. 10.6). It must be borne in mind that the size of the estimated effects is to some extent dependent upon the factors included and their categorization.

It was found that each of the factors included had a separate effect upon reading attainment after allowing for all the others. Social class can be seen to have by far the greatest effect. The difference between children from the middle classes (I, II and III non-manual

FIGURE 10.6: *Effects on mean reading score: (analysis of variance)*

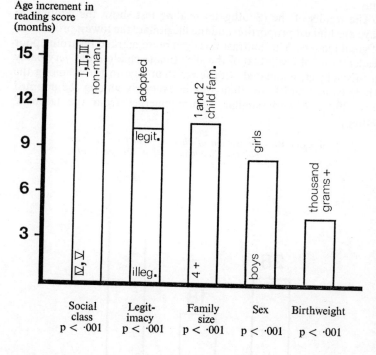

Age increment in
reading score
(months)

combined) and those from the manual social classes is equivalent to
nearly 17 months of reading age.

The difference in reading attainment between the illegitimate and
the legitimate samples is equivalent to 10 months of reading age; the
additional effect of having been adopted is equivalent to a further 2
months reading age, making a difference of 12 months between
illegitimate children who were or were not adopted.

Next in magnitude of effect comes family size. Having three or
more siblings is equivalent to the loss of nearly 11 months reading
age which is more than the average difference between boys and girls
(about eight months in favour of the latter).

Compared with the social class and legitimacy effects, the influence
of 1,000 grams of birthweight is relatively small (about five months
reading age) but nevertheless important.

In summary, the adopted children remain marginally the best
readers, even after allowing for their more favourable social class
distribution and for the fact that they have fewer brothers or sisters.

On the other hand, while the social class characteristics of the illegitimate group add considerably to their overall disadvantages in making satisfactory reading progress, important illegitimacy effects remain independent of social class, sex, family size or birthweight. Also, it looks as if subsequent environmental factors have more important, probably cumulative effects, than birthweight.

Arithmetic attainment

Like reading, this was assessed by two means, an objective test and the teacher's rating of each child's achievement on a five-point scale. The descriptions of the five categories ranged from 'extremely good facility with number, and/or mathematical concepts; grasps new processes very quickly, shows insight and understanding' to 'little, if any, ability in this sphere; shows virtually no understanding at all'.

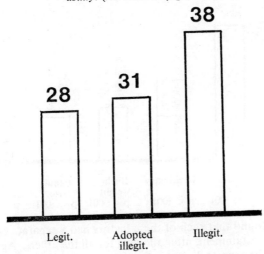

FIGURE 10.7: *Proportion of children with poor arithmetic ability: (test score 0–3) (per cent)*

The arithmetic test used was specially devised for our cohort study. It consists of ten problem arithmetic items, six of which have been previously used by the National Foundation for Educational Research with a similar age group.

The results of the test show the illegitimate group to have the highest proportion of low scores compared with the legitimate and the adopted (Fig. 10.7). Conversely, the latter two groups have a higher proportion of children with good scores (31 per cent, 31 per cent and 21 per cent). However, for once the performance of the adopted children is identical with that of the legitimate group and not superior to it, as has been the case regarding many of the other developmental aspects we have examined. From the analysis of the teachers' ratings, a very similar picture emerged.

Then the combined effects on problem arithmetic of the same five factors as for reading were examined: namely, social class; legitimacy status; family size; the child's sex; and his birthweight. The results are shown in terms of the gain in months of arithmetic age (Fig. 10.8).

FIGURE 10.8: *Effects on mean arithmetic score (analysis of variance)*

Age increment in problem
arithmetic score
(months)

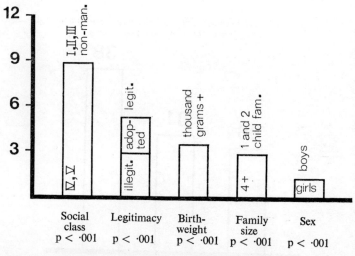

It was found that each of these factors had a separate effect upon arithmetic attainment, after allowing for all the others. Again, social class can be seen to have by far the greatest effect. The difference between children from the middle and manual classes respectively is equivalent to about nine months of arithmetic age.

The difference in arithmetic attainment between the illegitimate group on the one hand and the legitimate and adopted groups on the other hand is equivalent to five months of arithmetic age. Next in relative importance comes birthweight, an increase of 1,000 grams accounting for some four months of arithmetic age.

The effect of family size and of the child's sex are comparatively small (two months and one month of arithmetic age respectively).

In summary, the illegitimate children's performance in problem arithmetic remains the worst, even allowing for the effect of a number of social factors.

Special schooling

Teachers were asked whether in their view the pupil in question would benefit from special education. The highest proportion who were thought would benefit from such schooling was among the illegitimate (five per cent compared with two per cent among the legitimate and none in the adopted sample). This is what one would have expected in the light of the differences in abilities and attainments which were found between the three groups.

Changes of school

Since classroom organization, teaching methods and even standards of expectation vary considerably from school to school, frequent changes may have a detrimental effect on educational attainments. Having to adjust to the personality of different teachers and to make new friends, are additional factors liable to make a change of school an unsettling experience at best. Therefore, we examined whether during their two years at school, there were any differences in the number of schools attended by the legitimate, illegitimate and adopted samples.

About eight per cent of the illegitimate children had attended at least three different schools during their brief span of time in the infant school: this compared with three per cent of the legitimate group. A similar proportion of the adopted had experienced at least two changes of school; in their case it is likely, because of their favourable social class composition, that to some extent this high proportion was due to upward social mobility, i.e. fathers moving on to better jobs necessitating also moving house.

For children doing badly already, as was the case for the illegitimate group, frequent changes of school are likely to exacerbate further their existing learning difficulties. For the adopted, on the other hand, who were growing up in favourable circumstances and coping successfully with school work, one would expect many, if not all, to take in their stride changes of school and all that they involve.

Parental interest in their children's education

Of the measures of parental interest available in the whole study, the teacher's assessment of both the mother's and the father's interest in the child's educational progress was used. This was rated by teachers on a four-point scale, from 'very interested' to 'little or no interest'.

The highest proportion of mothers said to show little or no interest was found among illegitimate children and the lowest proportion among the adopted (29 per cent against four per cent); for the legitimate, the proportion was about midway between the other two groups (15 per cent). Conversely, the relatively largest number of mothers showing great interest was among the adopted (57 per cent), next came the legitimate (36 per cent) and the smallest proportion of very interested mothers was among the illegitimate (19 per cent).

These findings held true when analysed within the different social classes except for social class V (unskilled); here the proportion of mothers showing little or no interest was higher for legitimate than illegitimate children (Fig. 10.9). Among the adopted in this social class there was not even one mother showing lack of interest.

FIGURE 10.9: *Percentage of mothers assessed by teachers as showing 'no interest' in schooling—by social class*

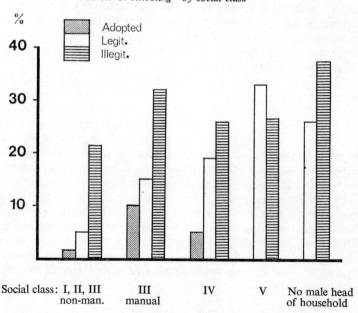

Turning now to paternal interest, there was in all three groups a sizeable proportion about whom the teachers could express no opinion—about a third among the legitimate and adopted and over half among the illegitimate. For those for whom teachers supplied ratings, the picture obtained mirrored that for the mothers of the three groups, the highest proportion of fathers showing great interest being the adoptive and the least those of the illegitimate. The converse was also true.

Analysing the findings separately for the five social class groupings, it was again among the fathers of the illegitimate where the proportion showing little or no interest was greatest with the exception of social class V (Fig. 10.10). Again, not one adoptive father in social class V was said to lack interest.

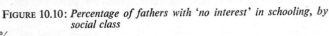

FIGURE 10.10: *Percentage of fathers with 'no interest' in schooling, by social class*

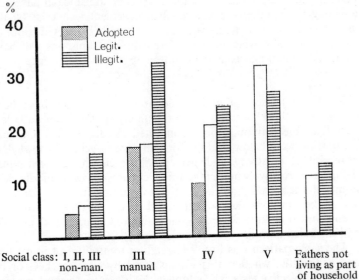

Effect of the child's family situation on attainment

On theoretical grounds one would expect that living with both his own parents would, generally speaking, provide a more stable and secure background for a child and thus be associated with better educational attainments. This assumption was confirmed in the National Child Development Study where it was found that children living in any kind of atypical family situation—i.e. other than being brought up by both their own parents—obtained a lower level of educational attainment (Pringle, Butler and Davie, 1966). Therefore one would have expected those illegitimately born children who were living with both their natural parents to do better than all the other groups. However, this was not the case. There was no evidence that children living with their own parents or in a two-parent family obtained better ratings or test scores than those living either with their own mother and her family, or with their mother only, or with neither parent; indeed, if anything, the opposite was true, lowest scores being obtained by children living with their natural parents. Nor did the latter show more interest in their children's educational progress than there was among any other type of family.

Since there were no social class differences between the different family situations, it looks as if the many problems and pressures, besetting all the families, were the overriding influence in adversely affecting the children's educational achievements—at least by the age of seven years. It remains to be seen whether this will continue to be the case or whether the different family situations will have some differential effects as the children approach adolescence.

Summary

In all the aspects of ability and attainment, which have been examined in this chapter, the illegitimate group did significantly less well than the legitimate or the adopted children. Thus a higher proportion were below average for their age in general knowledge, oral ability, creativity and perceptual development; even those living in the relatively more favourable circumstances of middle class homes did less well than the legitimate children from such homes. The highest performance was achieved by the illegitimate who had been adopted and this was particularly marked among those in semi- and unskilled homes.

The same pattern was found in relation to attainment in reading and arithmetic, whether this was assessed by class teachers or by means of objective tests. The adopted children were the best readers, next came the legitimate and the illegitimate did worst, being on average almost a year behind in reading level.

The fact that a higher proportion in the illegitimate group had also experienced a greater number of school changes probably constituted an additional handicap to their educational progress.

Then the interest shown by the parents in their children's educational progress was examined. Again, the proportion of both mothers and fathers showing little or no interest was highest among those of the illegitimate children and lowest among adoptive parents.

Lastly, the type of family situation in which the illegitimate children were living at the age of seven years made little difference. Contrary to expectation, the attainments of those living with both their natural parents were not higher than of those in other types of family situation. It remains to be seen whether any changes have taken place by the time the children approach adolescence.

CHAPTER ELEVEN
Behaviour and Adjustment

THE MAIN MEASURE used to assess the children's behaviour and adjustment in school was the Bristol Social Adjustment Guide. The overall results obtained for the illegitimate, adopted and legitimate samples will be compared and contrasted, and then the effects of social class, legitimacy status, family size, birthweight and sex of the child will be analysed.

In addition to an overall, global assessment, the Guides also make it possible to distinguish broad patterns of behaviour such as 'anxiety for acceptance by children', 'withdrawal' and 'depression'. These patterns or syndromes will also be explored.

Then regularity of school attendance, parental condoning of absences and attendance at child guidance clinics will be examined since they may provide some further pointers to the children's behaviour and adjustment.

The Bristol Social Adjustment Guides

The Guides were designed to measure the extent to which a child's behaviour in school deviates from normal. A large number of concrete descriptions of behaviour are presented to the teacher who is asked to underline any description which fits the pupil in question. Those aspects of behaviour which show some degree of deviance from normal are then identified and given a code or score. By adding together the number of coded items for each child, a total, overall score is obtained, which is a reflection of the child's emotional and social adjustment in school. The higher the score, the more deviant the behaviour noted by the teacher.

The designer of the Social Adjustment Guides (Stott, 1966) has adopted a grouping of these scores into three categories: 'stable' which denotes scores ranging from 0 to 9; 'unsettled' which is applied to scores from 10 to 19; and 'maladjusted' which is used for scores of 20 or more. Though this terminology and classification have not yet been shown to be necessarily applicable in, for example, a clinical context, they will be used here for the sake of comparability both with the whole cohort study and with the work of others (Davie *et al.*, 1971; Chazan, 1968).

Behaviour and adjustment in school

The proportion of children found to be 'maladjusted' among the illegitimate sample was much higher than among the other two groups (Table 11.1). In fact, the behaviour in school of one in every four of these children was so deviant from the normal as to be classified in this way. The adopted group, on the other hand, closely resembled the legitimately born in this respect.

TABLE 11.1: *Bristol Social Adjustment Guide Scores*

| TOTAL SCORE | ILLEGITIMATE | | LEGITIMATE |
	Not Adopted	Adopted	
	%	%	%
Stable (0–9)	47	64	65
Unsettled (10–19)	28	19	22
Maladjusted (20 +)	24	16	13

The differences between the groups cannot be explained on the grounds of sex differences. Though most studies—whether using the Guides or other assessment devices—show the incidence of maladjusted behaviour to be higher among boys, it will be recalled that there was a slightly higher proportion of girls in the illegitimate sample. If anything, this should therefore have worked in the opposite direction from that found. In fact, the contrary was the case: the proportion of 'maladjusted' children was nearly twice as high among the illegitimately as among the legitimately born. Sex differences were in the usual direction, boys exceeding girls (Fig. 11.1)

FIGURE 11.1: *Percentages of 'maladjusted' children for boys and girls*

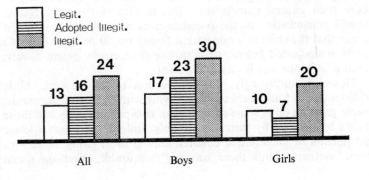

Legit.
Adopted Illegit.
Illegit.

| All | Boys | Girls |
| 13 16 24 | 17 23 30 | 10 7 20 |

FIGURE 11.2: *Percentages of 'maladjusted' children for social class*

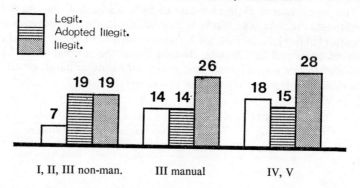

The difference in social class composition is a more likely explanation. A marked trend for the incidence of 'maladjustment' to increase the lower the social class was shown for the whole cohort (from six per cent in social class I to 22 per cent in social class V). Our results show that though the social class composition did have a marked effect, it did not entirely account for the high incidence of 'maladjustment' among the illegitimate sample. Within each of the different social class groupings, the illegitimate group contained a higher proportion of 'maladjusted' children; and, just as among the legitimate, the incidence was highest in the lowest social groups (Fig. 11.2).

Then the incidence of social maladjustment was examined in relation to the family situation in which the illegitimate children were living at the age of seven years. Given the similarity in social class composition and in the proportion of boys and girls in the different types of family situations, one would have predicted some differences. For example, one would expect a lower incidence of maladjustment among those children who had since birth lived with both their natural parents since this is akin to the most typical family constellation in the population as a whole; or one might argue that the child in a one-parent family would be more likely to show maladjusted behaviour than one from a two-parent family, even if only one was his natural parent.

However, surprisingly, this proved not to be the case. Little difference was found between those living with their natural parents, those growing up in some other type of two-parent family and those being brought up by their mother only. Indeed, there was a lower proportion of maladjusted children among those living alone with their mothers. Thus there was no measurable effect on social adjustment according to whether the child lived in a family situation very similar to that of the typical nuclear family or in some kind of atypical family situation.

Next, the combined effects on social adjustment of the following factors were studied: social class, sex, family size, birthweight and legitimacy status. The results are presented in terms of good or poor social adjustment. Because there is no comparable scale corresponding to the age scales available for assessing basic educational attainments (such as reading or arithmetic) it is rather more difficult to interpret the findings. Nevertheless, the results of this analysis follow a pattern similar to that described for reading. Social class was found to have the most marked effect, followed closely by the child's sex. Next comes legitimacy status whereas birthweight and family size can be seen to/have relatively less effect (Fig. 11.3). Thus social class and the child's sex have a much greater effect on social adjustment than whether the child is legitimate, illegitimate or adopted.

FIGURE 11.3: *Effects on Bristol Social Adjustment Guides score (analysis of variance)*

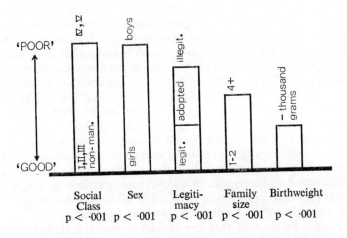

Syndrome scores

Until now, only a single, global measure of behaviour and adjustment in school has been used. Inevitably, this is relatively crude and undifferentiated since it does not distinguish between different kinds of deviant behaviour. For example, of two children with the same global score, one may be aggressive, restless and unco-operative whereas the other may be withdrawn, timid and anxious.

The design of the Guides makes it possible to distinguish these and other kinds of behaviour. Items of behaviour showing common features are grouped together in patterns or 'syndromes', such as 'withdrawal', 'depression' or 'hostility towards adults'. Every child has a score for each syndrome, ranging from 0 to whatever is the total possible score for that syndrome and these sub-scores—which are part of the global score for each child—are referred to as 'syndrome scores'. For each of the twelve syndromes, the average 'syndrome score' was analysed for the three samples (illegitimate, adopted, and legitimate) allowing for sex, social class, and family size differences. There were considerable differences between the legitimate, adopted and illegitimate groups for seven out of the 12 possible syndromes or behaviour patterns (*Table* A11.2).

Among the illegitimate children a relatively larger proportion than among the legitimate received high syndrome scores for showing 'Hostility to adults', 'Hostility to children', 'Unconcern for adult approval' and 'Inconsequential behaviour' (Children exhibiting such behaviour seem to have little or no regard for the consequences of their actions and their misbehaviour is frequent and recurrent).

A comparison between the patterns of syndrome scores obtained by the illegitimate and the adopted shows considerable similarities: among both groups a high proportion show 'Hostility to adults', 'Hostility to children', 'Inconsequential behaviour' and 'Restlessness'. On the other hand, only the illegitimate show 'Unconcern for adult approval' as a specific characteristic; syndromes of withdrawal ('Unforthcomingness, depression and withdrawal'), and 'Anxiety for acceptance by adults' were accounted for by factors such as social class and family size. Only the adopted show 'Anxiety for acceptance by children' as a specific characteristic of their group.

These findings suggest that for a sizeable minority of the illegitimately born children, including the adopted, relationships with teachers tend to be an area of conflict, characterized by a lack of concern for their approval or by hostility to them. The reasons why this should be so deserve further, more detailed study.

It must be stressed that the Guides pinpoint deviations from 'normal' school behaviour, which in effect means behaviour expected by teachers. Insofar as the school is basically a middle class institution and teachers themselves either come from, or have been 'educated into', this same social class, the behaviour expected from pupils inevitably corresponds to a considerable extent to middle class norms. At the same time, many of the deviations in social behaviour identified by the Guides are abnormal by any standard, and not merely or simply a reflection of school norms.

Regularity of school attendance

Since the health and physical development of our three groups were very similar, one would expect a similar attendance record on health grounds alone. However, other aspects are known to play a significant role. Perhaps chief among these are how happy the child's relationships are at school and how well he is progressing in comparison with his peers. But attendance is also closely affected by the child's relationships with his parents and their attitudes to him (Kahn and Nursten, 1968; Tyerman, 1968).

Viewed in this context, one would expect to find a markedly higher proportion of illegitimate children to have a poor attendance record. This was in fact the case (Table 11.2). There were twice as many illegitimate as legitimate children (11 per cent against five per cent) who put in less than 75 per cent of possible attendances.

TABLE 11.2: *School attendance and parental condoning of absence*

| SCHOOL ATTENDANCE | ILLEGITIMATE | | LEGITIMATE |
	Not Adopted	Adopted	
	%	%	%
Under 75%	11	7	5
76%–89%	32	30	28
90%	58	63	66
Parents condone absence	4	.5	1

Parental condoning of absences

This assessment is based on reports by the teachers of whether or not the parents of a child condoned his absences. The overall proportion of condoning parents was small—after all, quite a proportion of absences are likely to have been justified; only a minority would be due to reasons such as the child being needed at home to look after younger or sick members of the family or his actually truanting, about which parents may have known or half-known.

Nevertheless, marked differences were found between the illegitimate, adopted and legitimate groups, the highest proportion of condoning parents being among those of the illegitimate children (Table 11.2).

Attendance at child guidance clinics

For some years now and continuing today, such clinics have been in short supply and so lacking in staff that they have long waiting lists. Furthermore, the knowledge that this is so discourages referrals to them by teachers. Hence the number of children who have actually attended is likely to be only the tip of an iceberg of all those thought to require psychological and psychiatric help.

There is also some evidence to suggest that children from middle class homes are more likely to be referred to child guidance clinics than those from a working class background. This would lead one to expect that the illegitimate group would be under-represented and the adopted over-represented in view of their different social class compositions.

However, the picture is only partially as one would have predicted. On the one hand, a relatively higher proportion among the illegitimate (three per cent) than the legitimate (one per cent) attended such clinics; on the other hand, among the adopted sample the proportion was also higher than among the legitimate (two per cent).

Summary

Comparing the behaviour and adjustment in school of the legitimate, the adopted and the illegitimate children, the last mentioned show a higher incidence of difficulties than the other two groups. However, somewhat contrary to expectation, the actual family situation in which the seven-year-old illegitimate children were living, did not seem to have a differential effect on their adjustment.

Social class and the child's sex had the most marked effects, while family size and birthweight had relatively the least. Illegitimacy had an effect similar in size to that of sex differences. With regard to patterns or syndromes of deviant or 'maladjusted' behaviour, more illegitimate—and to a lesser extent more of the adopted, too—than legitimate children showed behaviour indicative of poor relationships with teachers.

Two other possible indicators of adjustment in school were examined, namely regularity of attending school and attendance at a child guidance clinic. In both respects the illegitimate differed from the legitimate group, the findings suggesting a higher degree of maladaptive behaviour among the former.

PART IV

THE CURRENT SCENE AND FUTURE PROSPECTS

CHAPTER TWELVE
Born Illegitimate—
Born Disadvantaged

An overview and interpretation

THE AIM OF THIS chapter is to summarize the major findings and to relate them to one another in an attempt to answer the questions asked at the beginning: how are illegitimately born children faring in the short- and in the long-term? Does illegitimacy continue to pose personal and social problems either to the mothers or to the children by the time they are seven years old? And how do children brought up by their own mothers compare with those who were adopted?

Before outlining the main findings and conclusions, two general points need to be made. It must be borne in mind, that as our title indicates, this is primarily a study of illegitimately born children and their development during the first seven years of life, rather than of the services which exist to help meet their needs or those of their mothers. Clearly these merit investigation. Almost every aspect or facet which we report on has implications for the mothers themselves which suggests that a companion study devoted primarily to their problems is desirable.

Another question we did not explore is the nature and effect of the stigma which apparently continues to be attached to illegitimacy. Although some reference is made to its effect on pregnancy management and child rearing, a thorough examination of these questions requires a differently designed study.

Standards for comparisons

The main yardstick for assessing development and progress was the whole cohort of children born in March 1958, of whom the illegitimate formed a part. Comparisons were also made according to the marital status of the mothers, both at the time of confinement and at the time of the follow-up when the children were seven years old. For the situation at birth a fourfold classification was used: first, whether or not the mother was cohabiting; and within each of these categories, whether she was single or had been married.

By the time the child was seven years, a six-fold classication was used to describe the family situation: where the child was being brought up in a two-parent family, three groups were distinguished namely both natural parents, one natural and a step- or adoptive parent or adoptive parents; where the child was living with his mother only, two groups were distinguished, namely where the mother was alone or lived with some other people; the sixth group consisted of children who lived with neither parent, either being with realations or in the care of the local authority or a voluntary organization.

At risk from the start

The mothers' background. There were no differences in social class background between mothers who were having a legitimate or an illegitimate baby respectively. However, this finding relates to her class of upbringing and not to the group to which she belonged either in her own right, according to her occupation during pregnancy or subsequently, or, alternatively, to that of the putative father or the man she cohabited with subsequently.

At the time of conception one would not expect the future mothers of illegitimate babies to show any marked disadvantage in comparison with mothers-to-be in the population at large since there was no difference in social class background. That this was the case is suggested by the fact that there was no difference in height between mothers of legitimate and illegitimate babies—height reflecting social class and also being regarded as one objective indication of level of reproductive efficiency.

Nevertheless, right from the outset illegitimately born babies were at a potential disadvantage in one respect: this is in relation to their mother's age and parity. The proportion of very young mothers was five times greater among the illegitimate than the legitimate and nearly twice as many of the former, or two-thirds of the sample, were mothers of first babies. The prevalence of low birthweight and the perinatal mortality rate are both higher among children of such mothers.

At the time of confinement the majority of the mothers of illegitimate babies were single, non-cohabiting women.

Ante-natal care. The three indicators, used to assess the care that mothers-to-be of illegitimate babies exercised during their pregnancy, clearly showed that a higher proportion than among the legitimate did not seek such care or did so later than was advisable. This unsatisfactory level of pregnancy management also extended to failure to make an advance booking for their delivery. Lack of adequate ante-natal care is also related to unfavourable pregnancy outcomes, including a higher mortality rate.

Birth hazards. The greatest—because final—of these are stillbirths and neonatal deaths. Among the illegitimate, the overall mortality rate was markedly higher.

Low birthweight (under 2,500 grams) is one of the most important 'high risk' factors and a higher proportion of the illegitimate fell into this birthweight group: moreover, the entire birthweight distribution among the illegitimate was less favourable than for the legitimate babies. This was due both to higher proportions being born too early or too late, and to a depression of foetal growth rates. Even when allowance was made for factors such as birthweight, a higher proportion of young mothers, the birth position of the illegitimately born baby and the mother's smoking habits during pregnancy, the mortality rate still remained higher than in the whole cohort.

So from conception onwards one can discern the complex and inter-acting network of adverse circumstances which begins to affect the illegitimately born child from the very start of his life. If he is to have an equal chance by the time he reaches school age, he would need to enjoy particularly favourable conditions, in his relationships, his home circumstances and his environment generally, to compensate him for his comparatively poor start.

Unfortunately, for the majority the opposite happened: the disadvantages continued in the years to come. Hence their combined and cumulative effect only served to heighten further the differences in development and adjustment between the illegitimate and the whole birth cohort. Could a favourable environment have halted or reversed the effects of early disadvantages and deprivations? And to what extent might it succeed in doing so? It became possible to examine these questions because about a third of the illegitimately born babies, who survived the perinatal period, were given up by their mothers for adoption, and at the age of seven years were living in much more favourable home environments than the group of children who had not been adopted.

The first seven years of life

The family situation. The majority of the illegitimately born were living in some kind of two-parent family by the time they were seven years old when those who were adopted are included. Though quite a high proportion were under the care of at least one of their own natural parents, a considerable number of children lived in a home which lacked a father figure. Only about one in four children lived with both their natural parents.

With respect to social class, considerable downward social mobility had occurred since birth among the mothers who had decided to keep their children. Whereas the social class of upbringing had been little different among the mothers-to-be of legitimate and illegitimate babies, in the intervening years a marked change had taken place. Compared with the legitimate sample, less than half the original proportion were now living in middle class homes. The contrast with the social background of those who were adopted was even more striking. Almost twice as many as in the whole cohort were living in middle class homes and this rose to over four times as many when compared with the illegitimate who remained with their mothers.

Thus, our findings confirm those of others that illegitimate children, who remain with their own mothers, are likely to grow up in a poorer social environment than is the case for the population as a whole. In addition, a high proportion were not only living in an atypical family situation but in many cases a stable or constant father figure was not available. Again, previous studies have shown that children in atypical homes are at greater risk of developing behaviour, learning and other difficulties because family relationships in such homes are more likely to be disrupted, disturbed or otherwise unsatisfactory.

For the whole cohort this finding was also confirmed; for example, children living in atypical family situations contained a higher proportion of poor readers (Pringle, Butler and Davie, 1966). However, such families also contained a higher proportion of working class homes and when comparisons were made within social class there were no differences in reading performance between children in social class IV and V whether or not the family situation was atypical, whereas such differences were present among children from middle class families.

This finding of a differential effect of atypical family situations in different social classes is open to a number of interpretations. Which is the correct one awaits further investigation. It might be that children in semi-skilled and unskilled working class homes are in many cases disadvantaged in so many ways, that the effects of the family situation as such cannot be readily isolated. Or it might be that there is still closer social coherence among lower working class families so that relatives, friends and neighbours more readily step into the breach by lending support when one parent is absent. Perhaps a combination of these conditions is at work and there may well be other possible reasons.

No differences were found in paternal occupational status of the illegitimate sample according to the type of family situation in which the children were living. Hence it was possible to consider whether there were differential effects on attainment and adjustment relating to the different types of family situation which existed among the sample.

Mothers going out to work. The majority of mothers who kept their illegitimate child worked outside their home before the child went to school and nearly half of them did so on a full-time basis. This proportion was much higher than among all the legitimate children; and among the adopted children the number of full-time working mothers dwindled to a mere three per cent. There was little change in this pattern after the children reached school age, except that by then a higher proportion of mothers among both the legitimate and the adopted accepted outside employment; however, even then it was predominantly on a part-time basis.

Whether a mother's accepting paid employment outside the home is necessarily detrimental to the child's well-being is a controversial issue on which opinions are far more plentiful than facts. It has become particularly topical in the past 10 to 15 years during which the proportion of married women workers with children has been steadily rising. Even research findings are so contradictory that almost any point of view finds support (Stoltz, 1960). Most likely this is due to failure to take into account all the relevant factors. Moreover, the factors may themselves have opposite effects. An analysis, carried out for the whole cohort, showed this quite clearly.

'Working mothers were more in evidence in the less skilled social class groups, so that on this basis their children might be expected to compare unfavourably in school performance with those of non-working mothers. However, working mothers tended to have smaller families and, as has been shown, children from small families do better at school than those in large families.' (Davie, Butler and Goldstein, 1971).

Because it had already been found in the whole cohort study that children living in atypical parental situations are at some disadvantage educationally, the analysis of the effects on children of mothers working outside the home was confined to those living with both natural parents. This analysis was designed so as to make allowance for social class and family size differences.

One other point remains to be made. Probably the most important, single factor which determines the effect on the child of the mother's working outside the home is the adequacy of the substitute care she is able to arrange for the time when she is absent. Though this is a most difficult aspect on which to obtain reliable quantitative or qualitative data, the need to do so is urgent. Unfortunately, our cohort could not supply any information on this vital issue: indeed, this kind of study is not appropriate for this purpose.

Family size. Marked and rather complex differences were found between the illegitimate, adopted and legitimate samples. There was a high proportion of only children among both the adopted and the illegitimate groups. The latter, however, contained also the highest proportion of very large families (six or more). Family size differed markedly among the illegitimately born according to the family situation, large families predominating where both of the child's natural parents were living together. One child families were highest among fatherless children and those who were not living with either of their natural parents.

There was, then, a higher proportion of both one child and large families in our sample than one would have predicted for an illegitimate group of this social class composition. For the whole cohort clear evidence was obtained that children from large families are at a considerable disadvantage at school. This inverse relationship between family size, and ability and attainment would be operating in opposing directions among the illegitimate sample: those from large families, suffering from yet a further environmental handicap, those from one child families doing relatively better.

Moving house. While moving house is a common enough experience for children, especially in our increasingly mobile society, nevertheless the more frequent the moves the more likely they are to prove an unsettling experience. If the move is to somewhere right outside the locality it makes matters worse because of the greater difficulty of maintaining relationships with former friends and classmates. For mothers of illegitimate children, the situation is likely to be even more difficult, partly because a high proportion are unmarried and partly because changes in family constellation are likely to involve a change of home.

This was found to be so. Overall, illegitimate children experienced a much more unsettled life than the legitimate. Mothers living in another household had the fewest moves, probably because their situation was accepted and they derived support, both moral and economic, from belonging to another family group. The highest number of moves occurred among two-parent families, where one parent only was the child's natural parent.

Household amenities and overcrowding. Looking at the physical environment of the illegitimately born, a very high proportion were disadvantaged, in comparison with the legitimate. Among the latter there was however a marked social class effect, children in social class V homes being more likely to lack or have to share the basic household amenities. There were no such straightforward social class effects nor were there any marked differences in the availability of basic amenities according to the different family situations in which the illegitimate children were living.

The most outstanding feature was the privileged position of the adopted children on the one hand, and the very high prevalence of shared or lacking amenities among the illegitimate on the other hand, it being twice as high as among the whole cohort.

Since there was a roughly similar proportion of large families among the legitimate and the illegitimate samples, one might expect to find a similar degree of overcrowding. Once again, however, the illegitimate were worse off despite the fact that the group contained also a high proportion of only children. Overcrowding was most severe among those children living with both their natural parents, probably because they had the highest incidence of large families. Among the adopted overcrowding was almost non-existent.

Few people would question that the quality of everyday life is profoundly affected by the availability of basic amenities such as indoor sanitation, hot water supply and some space for privacy as well as the pursuit of hobbies. Inevitably too it affects the temper of all members of the household, but particularly the mother's whose task is made so much more onerous by having to cope with lack of space and household amenities. Overcrowding may also result in poor or interrupted sleep which in turn is likely to affect a child's receptiveness in school and his ability to respond. It is worth recalling here that in a recent survey more than a third of the homeless were found to be one-parent families, showing also that their plight had not improved during the past ten years (Greve, Page and Greve, 1971).

The detrimental effects of poor household amenities and over-crowding upon educational performance and social adjustment in schools have been clearly demonstrated among the whole cohort.

'Those findings are particularly disturbing since poor housing conditions and overcrowding tend to "key in" with one another and with other disadvantaging circumstances. . . "Simply" building more houses is unfortunately not enough. . . . The housing problem is inextricably entwined with the "low-wage problem", the employment situation and the availability of public transport' (Davie, Butler and Goldstein, 1971).

Supplementary or substitute care. Inevitably, a considerable number of children experienced such care, not only because a high proportion of mothers worked outside the home but also because family circumstances were difficult and unsettled in many cases. Over three times as many illegitimate as legitimate children were placed in day care facilities.

Even this proportion is certainly an underestimate. In the first place, nearly two-thirds of the mothers of illegitimate children worked before they went to school yet only a quarter of the children were reported to have experienced day care; even allowing for relatives helping out, a sizeable discrepancy remains. Another reason is that no information was available on one type of substitute care, namely child minding, whether by officially registered minders or whether the mother had made some private arrangements.

No information was available either on the child minding arrangements entered into by mothers of all the cohort children. However, the proportion would almost certainly have been much smaller in their case since fewer mothers went out to work, particularly during the child's pre-school years.

There are grounds for believing that among all the different kinds of available day care, a high, if not the highest, proportion of unsatisfactory conditions for children's development is to be found among child minders. However, the mothers of illegitimate children, as indeed many other mothers who are forced by circumstances to seek outside employment, have little choice. 'There is an acute shortage of provision for the day and residential care of pre-school children in every area of the country ... The problem is always that many more children need facilities than there are facilities available' (Yudkin, 1967). In the intervening years very little has happened to improve the situation materially.

With regard to coming into the care of a local authority or voluntary body, the proportion of children who experienced this separation from home was five times higher among illegitimate than legitimate children. Again, one would expect this higher incidence because of the multiplicity of problems which beset the families, particularly mothers on their own.

Much evidence has accumulated during the past 20 years to show that 'prolonged institutional care during the early years of life leaves a child very vulnerable to later stress, if not already damaged intellectually and emotionally' (Dinnage and Pringle, 1967). More recently, a study of all the children in the cohort who had been in care for at least one period lasting four weeks or more, showed that as a group they were seriously disadvantaged quite apart from the fact of their removal from home (Mapstone, 1969).

There is little doubt that reception into care is inevitably a disturbing experience, particularly for the young child who is unable to understand the reasons for what is happening. This is so even when his life has previously been a happy and settled one. When the opposite has been the case, the experience is one more among several adverse factors likely to have a detrimental effect on his development.

In respect of almost every circumstance considered so far, it is evident that the illegitimately born children had the dice heavily loaded against them, being increasingly hampered by the inter-related strands of an intricate web of environmental hardships and deprivations. What then were the effects of these disadvantages on the children's physical, intellectual, educational and social development?

Effect on development, attainment and adjustment

Physical development. The incidence of physical defects was no greater among all the illegitimate than the legitimate children. This was true also for admissions to hospital for non-fatal accidents. Nor was there a higher prevalence of impairment of hearing and vision; and developmental milestones were reported to have been achieved at more or less the same time by both groups. That the illegitimate children's physical development was so satisfactory is a great tribute to their mother's care since in so many cases this must have been made infinitely more difficult by the conditions of hardship in which so many of the families were living.

Abilities and attainments. A number of tests and assessments were used to explore and compare the abilities and attainments of the illegitimate, adopted and legitimate groups of children respectively. Consistent and significant differences were found between them on all the aspects which were examined. Time and time again the illegitimate sample were at the bottom of the league table, be it for general knowledge, oral ability, creativity, perceptual development, reading attainment or arithmetical skills.

Even in the relatively more favourable environment of middle class homes, the illegitimate did less well than legitimate children from such homes.

A different way of expressing the differences found between the illegitimate, adopted and legitimate groups is to say that over and above social class effects, important 'illegitimacy effects' remain; in reading alone, they account for some 12 months of difference in progress between the adopted and the illegitimate samples, whereas similar progress had been made by the legitimate and the adopted. The evidence also suggests that environmental factors have more important and long-term effects than birthweight.

Once the illegitimately born children went to school, further dis-advantages were in store for them. Many recent studies have under-lined the important part which parental interest plays in promoting a child's scholastic progress and in developing favourable attitudes to learning in general. Regularity of school attendance clearly is an advantage and so is the chance of remaining at one school during the infant stage which after all usually only lasts for two years.

In all three of these aspects, the illegitimately born were at a disadvantage. A higher proportion of both their mothers and their fathers showed little or no interest in their educational progress compared with the parents of the legitimate and adopted children. Irregular school attendance was more characteristic of the illegitimate and they had also experienced a greater number of changes of school.

Behaviour and adjustment in school. Marked differences were found between the illegitimate and legitimate children. The fact that the incidence of maladaptive behaviour among the former was much higher was partly due to social class differences though these did not entirely account for it. Contrary to expectation, however, little difference was found between children living with their natural parents, those growing up in some other type of two-parent family, and those being brought up in atypical family situations. However children living with their mother only, tended to show a greater degree of social adjustment. This suggests that enjoying a mother's undivided attention is relatively beneficial, at least up to the age of seven years.

Probably it is in the nature of the Bristol Social Adjustment Guides that one should seek the reasons why social class seemed relatively so influential a factor while the type of family situation appeared to be of little importance. The Guides focus on the way the child behaves in school towards his teacher and the other children, and on the extent to which this behaviour deviates from normal class room behaviour. Hence the Guides measure adaptation, and indeed conformity, to school norms. This means that what is considered 'normal' is by and large the kind of behaviour and responses expected by what is basically a middle class institution—invented, it has been said, by the clever for the clever. Also since the Guides predominantly measure social behaviour, they are all the more likely to pinpoint social class differences. At the same time, many of the items denoting deviant behaviour would be considered abnormal by any standard and in any setting.

It is, of course, difficult to see how it could be otherwise. Teachers inevitably use group norms not only because they have to work in a group setting for most of the time but also because the success of their work depends to a considerable extent on the degree to which they can enlist their pupils' acceptance of these norms. What matters most perhaps is whether the teacher can distinguish, and hence treat differently and appropriately, the idiosyncratic individualist, the incipient rebel, the able misfit, the maladjusted failure and the disadvantaged deprived child who is rejected; more difficult still, whether he can recognize and help the child who is a mixture of some of these. In so far as the Guides go some way towards differentiating between the different types of maladaptive behaviour, thus far do they represent a step forward in mapping out, as it were, a profile of the child's behaviour and adjustment within the school setting.

The effects of environment

Though controversy continues regarding the relative contribution of heredity and environment to children's abilities, attainments and adjustment, it is widely accepted that heredity must play some role, even if only in setting an upper limit to potential development. That environmental influences inevitably play a major—some would say *the* major—part in determining the rate of learning and of the eventual ceiling of realized potential, is generally accepted by now. As far as could be determined by our relatively crude data there was little difference in the social class origins of the illegitimately born and the legitimate sample. Hence poorer heredity cannot be taken to account for the poorer performance of the former, at least as far as their mothers were concerned.

Admittedly, very little or nothing was known about the fathers so some of the differences may lie in that direction. There were, however, marked environmental differences betwen the illegitimate and the legitimate sample. If one takes just two examples: the fact that a high proportion of mothers had to work outside their home before the child went to school, would mean in most cases that the time available for playing and talking with the children was much more limited than that of mothers in the same socio-economic group. Furthermore as a group, the mothers of illegitimately born babies showed a marked downward social mobility so that subsequent to their confinement they compared unfavourably in social class grouping with the legitimate.

In contrast, the illegitimately born who had been adopted achieved in most aspects a standard as good as, and in some areas even higher than, the legitimate sample; and they were much superior to the illegitimate who had remained with their own mothers. Moreover, and again in contrast to the illegitimate group, the adopted children did consistently better even when they were being brought up in manual class homes than their counterparts in the whole cohort.

This apparent reversal of the usual social class trend is quite remarkable but can be understood in the light of the atypical and almost diametrically opposed situation of each of the two groups of children. Many of the stressful conditions and environmental handicaps which affected the illegitimate children as a group, were at work even in homes designated as middle class according to the breadwinners' occupation; hence they exerted a 'depressing' effect on the abilities and attainments of the children being reared in them.

Adopted children

Adopted children, in contrast, are taken into a family as an act of deliberate choice. The desire to adopt is often realized only after considerable periods of anxiety and waiting during which the prospective parents are assessed as to their suitability—a testing procedure most ordinary parents are not even aware of. Having succeeded in obtaining a child, he is likely to be cherished and a great deal of interest will be taken in his progress and achievements.

The baby too is subjected to a very rigorous selection procedure prior to adoption. Furthermore, it will be recalled that adoptive families tended to be small (82 per cent having two children only). So the atmosphere and attitudes in the home are likely to be more favourable than is usual whatever a family's socio-economic background, but perhaps particularly in working class homes. Hence it might be argued that the adoption process brings together exceptionally 'good' homes and exceptionally healthy, well-developed babies; and therefore a particularly favourable outcome in terms of child development is only to be expected.

Such a picture is, however, too rosy as well as an oversimplification. It ignores not only the inherent complexities and subtleties but also the fact that adoption involves strains and stresses peculiar to it. These have been considered in some detail in the light of research findings (Pringle, 1966) and some of the main considerations are relevant to this discussion.

To begin with, the inability to have children is for many couples a source both of sorrow and reproach (Humphrey, 1969). If a sense of personal inadequacy persists in either partner, this is bound to affect their attitude to each other and also, directly or indirectly, to the child. To the extent that adoption is still used as a supposed 'remedy' for neurotic women (and there is no evidence whether or not this continues to be the case) to that extent there would be a greater prevalence of neurotic mothers among adopted than ordinary children.

Nor is there any evidence to show whether it is still true that 'many adopters want a perfect child: female, of course beautiful, clever, a social success, who will pass examinations with ease' (Edwards, 1954). Even if such expectations are now less common, they are nevertheless likely to have harmful effects on the object of any such unrealistic hopes. All the more so when developmental tests, administered during early infancy, are now known to have very limited predictive validity.

There are two further pressures which inevitably affect adoptive parents. The first is disapproval of illegitimacy. Though it may be lessening, though it may not always be explicit or even conscious, this in no way detracts from its potency. As long as it exists in the community, neither the adopted child nor the adoptive parents can entirely escape its influence even if they themselves do not share the prejudice. Secondly, adoptive families are a minority group and so can count less on the understanding and support of their relatives and friends.

The children themselves are also likely to be more vulnerable. Indeed, it has been asserted that 'adoptive parents must be more prepared for failure than natural parents' (Moncrieff, 1961). Among likely reasons are some which have been reported in this study, showing that to be born illegitimate is to be born 'at risk'. The majority of children who become available for adoption have been conceived out of wedlock and are carried by mothers whose personal and family life is likely to be beset by problems; the very problems which make her consider parting with her baby. Recent psychological research suggests that 'pregnancy stress'—whether physical, emotional or both—can have adverse effects even while the baby is still in the uterus.

There is also evidence that even extremely young infants are sensitive to 'emotional atmosphere' and stress. For different reasons both the mother who relinquishes her child and the prospective adopters have to cope with many more doubts and anxieties than are faced by the 'normal' family. So the baby given up for adoption is likely to have been exposed to an anxiety-laden atmosphere in the early months of his life. During this time, too, he may have experienced one or more breaks and changes in mothering while he is awaiting adoption.

Thus it may well be that, during the early months at any rate, adopted children experience greater stress than those who stay with their own mothers; while in other respects they share the vulnerability of all illegitimately born children. Therefore our findings regarding the development of adopted children at the age of seven years are all the more remarkable. Their favourable home background succeeded in counteracting not only the effects of their unfavourable pre-natal conditions, but also the potentially harmful consequences of their disturbing experience during the earliest months of life.

Here then is the answer to the question posed previously: a favourable environment can halt or even reverse the effects of early disadvantages and deprivations. At least this was clearly the case by the time the adopted children reached the age of seven years. It remains to be seen what their later development will be like; and in particular whether adolescence proves a more difficult period. Of course, the same question applies to the children who remained with one or both of their parents.

Difficulties in learning and adjustment

There is one other link or relationship which must be stressed. This is the close and continuous interaction between learning difficulties and maladjustment, whether emotional or social. Potentially each can cause the other but in practice they often go hand in hand. What is still in question is the extent to which this is so which depends in turn on questions of definitions and borderlines. Some further light on this issue has been shed in the study of the whole cohort where it is argued that 'the results strongly indicate that in a substantial proportion of backward readers, maladjustment is a cause or an accompaniment of the backwardness rather than a result of it'. (Davie, Butler and Goldstein, 1971).

The relevance of this conclusion to our findings lies in recognizing the multi-faceted nature of the handicaps which afflicted the group of illegitimately born children we have studied. The fact, at first glance unexpected, that the type of family situation in which the child was living, did not seem to affect his social adjustment, may be a reflection of this.

It parallels an earlier finding, namely that whereas reading attainment was found to be significantly poorer in the cohort as a whole for children living in an atypical family situation (i.e. not with both natural parents), the exceptions to this were those belonging to social class IV and V (Pringle, Butler and Davie, 1966). The interpretation suggested then, may also apply here: that children in our sample were disadvantaged in so very many ways and their lives were beset by so many uncertainties and upheavals, that the actual type of family situation in which they were living made only a very marginal difference to the security and stability of their lives, and to their adjustment in school. Or else that in lower working class homes atypical family situations are more readily accepted and mutual support is more readily forthcoming, thus making problems less acute. Or possibly a combination of these factors is at work.

Retrospect and prospect

Inevitably many questions remain unanswered about exactly how the various aspects we have considered relate to and interact with one another. Inevitably too, there are many facets of the child's development and of his family background, especially in relation to the personality of his mother and other members of his household, on which we had no information at all. In particular, it is upon the subtler, more intangible aspects of what being born illegitimate and growing up in atypical family situations meant to the children, that we have been unable to shed any light. Nor can we say at present whether the problems encountered by this group of children differ, and if so in what respects, from those facing children who live for shorter or longer periods in one-parent families for reasons other than illegitimacy. However, a study of such children is now being undertaken, which will provide some comparative information (National Children's Bureau, 1971).

There is another set of questions, of equal, if not greater importance. The results we have presented give the overall situation of a whole group of children in terms of average patterns and performances. Concealed within this picture are the extremes—those children and their families who fared either exceptionally well or very badly.

One would expect, for example, that a stable, well-educated woman of 25 with some professional training might well be able to provide a satisfactory environment for her child even though he lacks a constant father figure; at least, she is more likely to do so than say a 17-year-old, backward girl who may well marry or live with the child's father but where the financial situation is precarious, where further children follow in quick succession and where family life is characterized by frequent quarrels and walk-outs by one or other parent. Of a different order still would be the difficulties of the child who grows up in a rather ill-defined family group where he thinks of his grandmother as his mother, of his mother as his sister, and of the changing procession of male figures as uncles or fathers, confusing relationships being matched by shifting economic fortunes.

It could be argued that it is even more important to find out about those who triumphed over adverse circumstances than those who were barely able to cope with or were completely overwhelmed by their multiple problems. Trying to clarify such questions should greatly further our understanding of possible preventive measures as well as shed much needed light on social and psychological pathology.

However, all such questions cannot be answered by a national longitudinal study alone. This must be supplemented by research methods employing more sophisticated, sensitive and complex tools and measures. On the other hand, studies such as ours provide not only comparative findings between 'normal' and special groups of children; they also chart a broad map which can then be filled in by more detailed and intensive investigations.

Meanwhile, material has been collected on the whole cohort when the children were 11 years of age. Thus it will be possible to follow-up the fate of both the illegitimately born who remained with their parents as well as those who were adopted, comparing the progress each group has made and exploring whether and how this differs from the whole cohort. Moreover, it is hoped that funds will be forthcoming to continue monitoring the development of all the children until they have left school and are launched into the adult world. After all, the crucial test of how well we have succeeded as parents, as teachers and as a society in caring for our young is how they themselves make out as parents, citizens and workers.

How far do the circumstances, practices and experiences of the mothers of illegitimate babies, described in this study, arise from the social climate and economic conditions which prevailed between their confinement in 1958 and the years up to 1965? To what extent have events meanwhile overtaken them? If there have been changes, how widespread are they and what is their nature? Are they mainly changes in attitudes or have there also been some changes in opportunities to lead a less disadvantaged life?

Regrettably, we do not know the answers to these questions. Any guess which one might hazard, based on the limited factual information which has been published in recent years on one-parent families, suggests that at least in their practical effects what changes there may have been, have had little positive impact on the plight of such families (Holman, 1970). The public admission by prominent and relatively affluent women that they are choosing to bring up their illegitimate children by themselves, can have little immediate impact, even if in the long run it were to contribute towards change. Indeed, in the short run, it may do harm by presenting to immature and unstable girls a glamorized and unrealistic picture of single-handed motherhood.

What then are the practical implications of our findings for case work with unmarried mothers? Many will say that they indicate that adoption is the right 'solution' for most illegitimate children; and that in their interest some pressure on the mother to follow this course of action is justified. Yet others feel strongly that such pressure is reprehensible and that each mother must be helped to come freely to the decision which seems best to her.

In our view the decision should be guided by 'the principle that the long-term welfare of the child should be the first and paramount consideration' (Departmental Committee on the Adoption of Children, 1970). It is a sobering thought that in what has been called the century of the child this principle has officially been suggested for the first time in 1970 as the right one for determining one aspect of social policy in relation to children and adults concerned with their care. Is it too much to hope that by the end of the decade this principle will be accepted as the basis for all policy and practice concerning children?

Nevertheless it would continue to be difficult to make balanced and far-sighted enough decisions even then, because the great variety of human situations does not allow of easy, ready-made solutions. This applies as much to unmarried mothers and their children as it does to all the other circumstances in which the help of social workers is sought. While it is professionally unacceptable to exert pressure, it is similarly unacceptable to fail to take into account current social conditions and their effects on children's development. Trying to bring about improvements in these conditions is one thing; making children suffer for outworn theories such as 'the importance of the blood tie' or the 'natural mother's inevitable superiority in caring for her child' is quite another.

To the questions we posed at the outset, fairly clearcut answers were found. Does illegitimacy still pose personal and social problems? Our findings show that it does and they give many indications as to their nature. How did the children fare from conception to the age of seven years? Overall, they were beset by a multiplicity of unfavourable circumstances which not only gave them a relatively poorer start in life but which continued to build up into a complex web of cumulative and interacting disadvantages and deprivations. Thus at the present time, to be born illegitimate is still to be born disadvantaged.

Perhaps this makes a fitting ending to this overview of the main findings. Our society may have become more permissive in no longer necessarily condemning as 'sinful' extra-marital sexual relations. 'Yet the more permissive sexual life of adults, which is a fact, has to be reconciled with the need of children for stability, which is another fact' (*The Times*, 1971). Meanwhile, illegitimately born children still continue in a very real and literal sense to suffer from the 'sins' of their fathers (and mothers)—at least, in all aspects which we were able to examine in our study. If punishing the innocent offspring of adult behaviour is no longer acceptable to an enlightened and humane society, which takes pride in treasuring its children, then we must prepare for fairly drastic changes in our national priorities. What these might be is discussed in the last chapter.

CHAPTER THIRTEEN

Present Paradoxes - Future Options

Looking beyond research

IN THIS, our final chapter, we shall be ranging beyond the confines of our study's findings to consider some of the main preventive measures needed to help children escape the unfavourable consequences of being born illegitimate. In doing so, broad issues of both policy and practice must inevitably be taken into account. Our viewpoint is based on a principle to which lip service has for long been paid but which is only slowly accepted in everyday practice and in law; namely, that the long-term interests, development and well-being of the child should be the first and overriding consideration.

As a society we continue to make paradoxical choices and to have paradoxical priorities. Hearts can be transplanted but the common cold cannot be cured; in 1968 more children died in fires alone than people were murdered, yet just one intensive and prolonged murder hunt probably costs more than the amount spent annually on teaching parents about fire risks and prevention; the supplementary allowance received by unsupported mothers for their children is substantially less than it would cost if substitute residential care had to be provided for them which, additionally, is known to be potentially harmful, especially for pre-school children; while much prominence is given to minority groups, such as delinquents, little is heard about the thousands of children who in our relatively affluent society grow up emotionally neglected and intellectually stunted.

Among them a high proportion of those born illegitimate will be found. In many ways their needs are similar to those of other disadvantaged children, especially all those growing up in one-parent families. Hence, most of the suggestions made in what follows are not specific. Furthermore, we shall largely omit from consideration those illegitimately born children who are adopted, since they escape—thanks to their favourable home background—the disadvantages which beset those babies who remain with their mothers.

The keynote must be prevention. Two essential measures are required one short- and the other long-term. First, what is already known needs to be applied now. Secondly, there is an urgent need to find out more. Little is known about the value or results achieved by preventive measures already available. Also new approaches must be devised and their application monitored so that their effectiveness can be evaluated.

Primary prevention

The aim here is to reduce the incidence of illegitimacy, using the term in the sense of unwanted pregnancies among single women. Where having a child outside marriage is a matter of deliberate choice, wider social and psychological issues are raised which lie outside the scope of our discussion.

There is little doubt that social stigma continues to be attached to illegitimacy, as does the view that women finding themselves in this position must expect to suffer the consequences of their action. In addition, single mothers share the economic and emotional hardships experienced by all groups of unsupported mothers (Wimperis, 1960; Wynn, 1964; Marsden, 1969; Holman, 1970). But whereas widows and deserted wives are likely to be given sympathy and support by relatives and friends, the unmarried mother often has to cope without either.

Preparation for parenthood. If this is the reality of the current situation, then clearly preventive measures have a part to play. The most effective educative measure is likely to be aimed at adolescents. What is required is neither a narrow course seen as a branch of biology or domestic science, primarily for girls, nor a very wide, general one in citizenship. Instead all schools should include in their curriculum a course in human relationships and child development, with particular emphasis on what is now known about the importance of the earliest years of life for optimal physical, emotional and intellectual growth.

The second measure is to make contraceptive advice and facilities much more readily available to young people. Such a proposal raises the fear that in consequence promiscuity will increase. There is little evidence that this would inevitably be so, but it seems in any case a justified risk in view of the alternative option. This is to have unwanted children remain the victims: some growing up unloved or rejected altogether; the majority being reared in adverse environmental conditions which may then have long-term detrimental consequences in later life. As a result an (at present unknown) number will grow into the alienated adults or inadequate parents of tomorrow. Inevitably too, society then shoulders part of the long-term burden, however reluctantly and cheese-paringly, in terms of meeting the cost of unemployability, mental illness and law-breaking, as well as of a new generation of children who have emotional and learning difficulties.

Premature parenthood is undoubtedly an important contributory factor to this vicious circle. Commonsense would suggest that very young parents, themselves not yet fully mature emotionally, are less able to provide the emotional support and intellectual stimulation so vital to a child's optimal development. Also, being at the beginning of their working life, financial and housing problems are likely to be additional difficulties. The results from our study lend support to this view. The fact that unplanned and unwanted pregnancies occur among married as well as unmarried couples only underlines further the value of early educative and preventive measures.

Equal opportunities and responsibilities for women. In the long run two other, and much more fundamental, social changes which are beginning to look less remote than they did even a few years ago, may bring about a radically altered situation. Their realization would entirely transform not only the lot of illegitimately born children but of all fatherless and otherwise socially disadvantaged children. The first is a single labour market for men and women offering equal opportunities and equal pay. This in turn would require adequate provision of supplementary day care, as well as of training and retraining facilities for women at different stages of their life.

The immense increase in the rate of maternal employment during the past 30 years has already produced a new situation: there are now working mothers in all types of families and in all social classes. In consequence there is a new and growing mass demand 'for a high-quality child care program, differentiated according to children's developmental needs, not a casework service for disturbed or disadvantaged parents ... There is no intrinsic reason why such a supplementary child care program should have a pejorative coloration or carry a stigma of parental inadequacy. The conditions of contemporary life have created the need for a new institution: widely available, professional child care centres' (Ruderman, 1968). This recommendation from the USA applies with equal force to the situation here.

The second is perhaps an even more fundamental change. This is to give practical recognition to the fact that children are society's investment in the future. A woman who devoted herself, full- or part-time, to their care would be entitled to appropriate wages, whether she is married or not; these might well be recoverable from the child's father but the onus for doing so should be on the state and not on the mother.

Both these changes would, indirectly, tend to lessen the stigma of illegitimacy because in this way women would have financial independence and security as of right; it would also be a concrete recognition of the fact that motherhood and adequate child rearing constitute a responsible and arduous task, undertaken in the interest of society, and demanding great skill and knowledge, quite apart from physical stamina and long hours.

Once such changes in the role and responsibilities of women and mothers have permeated the fabric of society, it will become possible to disentangle the complex strands—economic, social and emotional —which affect the development of illegitimately born children. For example, the effects of growing up fatherless or of experiencing 'multiple fathering' need to be studied within the context of a society in which it is thought desirable to blur the traditional and stereotyped sex roles; and whether or not illegitimacy has its own pathology in terms of both the mother's and the child's problems.

Perhaps one of the major difficulties about giving primary prevention the necessary priority in the allocation of funds is, that in a literal sense, there is nothing to show for it: just as an accident which has not happened, so a child from a disadvantaged, vulnerable family who is not backward or maladjusted does not appear in any statistics. Another difficulty is that primary prevention is essentially a long-term process because it depends as much on changing long-standing attitudes and behaviour as it does on changing society's laws and institutions. Hence it probably takes a generation to achieve significant improvements in the incidence of behaviour difficulties and learning problems. Meanwhile, measures for secondary and tertiary prevention need to be introduced to alleviate some of the present disadvantages of being born illegitimate and to reduce the prevalence of permanent damage.

Secondary prevention

Our findings have shown that, practically from conception onwards, illegitimately born children are vulnerable. Many other groups of socially disadvantaged children share this vulnerability and hence the measures suggested here do not essentially differ from those required for all other vulnerable groups (Pringle, 1965 and 1969). Their aim is threefold: to help families through periods of temporary strain and crisis; to improve, and where necessary, supplement the quality of care and education provided for children considered to be 'at risk'; and to prevent the disintegration of the family unit.

Because environmental deprivation affects development at an early age, and because it is cumulative, intervention must start early too. This means that the pre-school and early school years are a crucial time for introducing preventive measures and enrichment programmes. The various schemes being currently tried out in community development projects, educational priority areas, urban aid programmes and family advice services (Leissner, 1967; Leissner, Herdman and Davies, 1971), are all a beginning in this direction. But only the merest beginning. For example, 'the £3 million allocated to educational priority areas represents less than three week's expenditure on Concorde. Yet in spite of the technical complexities involved in building a supersonic airliner, the problems underlying the intellectual development of thousands of disadvantaged children are a great deal more complex and intractable' (Wiseman, 1970).

Early intervention. The keynote, then, must be early and constructive intervention. Early because problems rarely spring into being fully fledged, nor does the maladjusted or backward child do so. Constructive in the sense that intervention should aim at enabling the child or family to cope again independently as soon as possible. How this is most effectively done, still requires further experiment and study. But again, beginnings have been made.

To start with, available statutory services tend to be used least by those who have the greatest need. This was found to be the case for the whole birth cohort (Davie, Butler and Goldstein, 1971) and was confirmed by our results—for example, the limited and late use of ante-natal care. The reasons for this are probably compound and must be sought in the accessibility of services, both in terms of physical siting, and of psycho-social rapport and communication between disadvantaged families and the professional staff concerned. This situation should not be allowed to continue. For example, a domiciliary component to all child care and welfare facilities may help to ensure their greater use in areas of greatest need.

In the case of unmarried mothers there are likely to be additional barriers to seeking professional advice and help since this usually entails revealing their personal situation. Yet they are clearly in very great need of such help from the outset. Better pregnancy management is essential for all illegitimately born babies, whether or not they are subsequently adopted. What can be achieved in reducing, for example, the perinatal mortality rates among high risk mothers, has been strikingly shown by Sir Dugald Baird (1952 and 1969).

Counselling and casework. Next, counselling services and case work help should be readily available to the mother-to-be to help her take a dispassionate view of what is likely to be the best course in the child's long-term interest. It means taking into account all her circumstances, including her own attitudes to life in general, her hopes and ambitions, her anxieties and weaknesses, as well as practical issues such as the opportunities for accommodation, employment and supplementary child care available in the area where she will be living. At the same time, she requires concrete help with her immediate practical needs. Otherwise, she may be too preoccupied and overwhelmed by them to give her mind to planning ahead.

Even if she decides on adoption, the counselling service should remain available to her as long as the mother wants to avail herself of it. Not only will this ensure a happier early environment for the baby leaving its mother, since she herself will be less disturbed and confused; it might also contribute to her eventually becoming a more successful, because better adjusted, mother when she has a family at some later stage.

Financial support. The other main area in which secondary preventive measures are essential is the provision of adequate financial support. Basically this is common to all fatherless families though again the illegitimate probably fare worst. Financial hardship, accommodation difficulties, lack of suitable employment, insufficient and often inadequate day care facilities—these are the burdens borne by such families. They have been well-documented during the past ten years. Probably this evidence contributed to the decision to set up a commission to consider the needs of all one-parent families (The Finer Committee established by the Department of Health and Social Security in 1969).

Among proposals put forward to meet financial hardship is a fatherless-child standard allowance. If the mother is working her earnings should be disregarded; where she is not, a minimum maintenance allowance should also be available to her. Both the child's and the mother's allowance should be related to the current level of payment made to foster parents as well as to the cost of living index. These allowances might be made recoverable from the father according to his income but the responsibility for doing so might lie with the Inland Revenue.

Such a procedure is already in operation in Denmark, the father being expected to support his child until the age of 18, or 24 years if he continues in full-time education. It is a sad reflection of the lack of concern among our (predominantly male) legislators that, in the spring of 1971, a private member's bill, introducing such a provision, did not even secure a first reading because not enough Members of Parliament could be persuaded to re-enter the chamber, though enough were present in the House! Yet Canada already has anti-discrimination legislation in all its provinces, prohibiting different pay rates based on sex. Furthermore, the recently published report of a Canadian Royal Commission set up in 1967 contains the following recommendations: a guaranteed income from the state for the head of all one-parent families with dependent children; the prohibition of 'sex' and 'marital status' as grounds for discrimination in employment; and a determined effort to encourage women to move out of traditionally female occupations (Royal Commission on the Status of Women in Canada, 1970).

Perhaps we also need a Royal Commission on anti-discrimination? 'The differential between men's and women's wages, coupled with the scarcity of occupations in which a woman can adequately perform both an economic and maternal role, means that it is extremely difficult for a woman other than one who has had a professional training to earn a "living" wage' (Edwards and Thompson, 1971). This has led to the suggestion of training schemes especially designed for mothers of fatherless families so that those who wish to and are able to do so may become self-supporting (National Council for the Unmarried Mother and her Child, 1971).

Accommodation. Because many, if not most unmarried mothers are unable to compete for rented accommodation in the open market both for social and financial reasons, various schemes have been suggested to meet their need for low cost housing. Among these is the allocation by local authority housing departments of a proportion of reconditioned accommodation, integrated within the community; another idea is to make some type of collective provision, whether flats or houses, with shared facilities, e.g. a canteen, launderette, creches, nursery groups, as well as a housemother who can supervise older children when they return from school or who is able to baby sit to give the mother an occasional evening out.

Such a scheme might also contain temporary provision to help mothers adapt themselves to the role of a single handed parent and to provide a temporary haven in times of crises. Despite its obvious merits, group housing schemes have the disadvantage of confining young women in a segregated, all-female community which could easily become even more socially isolated as a result of being conspicuous in, and possibly ostracized by, the immediate neighbourhood. Nevertheless, these ideas deserve a trial with a built-in evaluation of their effectiveness.

Coping with the stigma. There are additional problems faced by the mother of an illegitimate child due to the stigma still attached to her condition. She may have to bear the prejudice of her own family, her friends and acquaintances. If she decides to seek anonymity in a large town, she will be facing yet greater loneliness and social isolation. Additionally, landladies and prospective employers are likely to be even less sympathetic to her than to other unsupported mothers with a small baby. All these problems, including the continuing stigma—the existence of which has prematurely been called in question by some—have been confirmed in a recent study. Moreover little evidence was found of any changes in the situation during the preceding decade (Holman, 1970).

To share some of these specific difficulties with others similarly placed, may provide some support. This idea might be worth exploring and evaluating by means of a specific service, using group discussions for mothers willing to participate. Some Social Service Departments are already using this method. Through it a broader kind of health education could also be provided, in addition to the comprehensive ante- and post-natal care recommended earlier. The need for this is suggested by, for example, the finding that where there is some degree of family stress there is a greater risk to the child of accidents in the home and on the roads.

Provision for the children themselves. A wide and flexible range of pre-school provision is required to replace the makeshift, inadequate and in some instances detrimental, substitute child care arrangements currently in use. They should aim to enrich and supplement rather than simply 'mind'. The more disadvantaged and deprived the child, the more skilled and trained the personnel must be if this aim is to be realized.

The same considerations apply once the child reaches school age. The illegitimately born will benefit from the type of class and school organization which is child-centred and flexible enough to cater for the needs of each individual pupil whatever his abilities and attainments. Also, like other children from one-parent families, they require an 'extended school day' to be safely but constructively and challengingly occupied till the parent returns home. Hobby clubs, preferably self-governing, adventure play grounds and constructive holiday provision are among the facilities which are of value as well as enjoyed by children.

In summary, then, the aim of secondary prevention should be to provide a broad and flexible range of educational and community programmes to counteract or minimize the ill-effects from which vulnerable children are prone to suffer: in this way one would hope to prevent their becoming educationally backward, emotionally disturbed, or both.

Tertiary prevention

At least a proportion of children exposed to an unsettled, insecure or stressful home environment will become emotionally maladjusted, educationally backward or both. That this is the case is again confirmed by the findings of our study. Similarly, children who have to live apart from their own families for long periods, or permanently, often develop behaviour and learning difficulties.

Tertiary prevention seeks to counteract, mitigate and, if possible, rehabilitate the emotionally disturbed, the intellectually deprived and the educationally underfunctioning child. Treatment aims to arrest and reverse unfavourable responses, and to prevent lasting damage to the child's capacity to make mutually rewarding relationships and to his ability to go on learning.

Do the needs of the illegitimately born differ from those of other children whose problems also include on the one hand, being exposed to ambivalent parental feelings or even rejection, and on the other hand, feeling a sense of shame about their parents, confusion about their family relationships and the absence of a stable, dependable father figure? This question awaits further study. Meanwhile, the same day and residential treatment facilities, as are available for all children suffering from emotional and educational problems, are required. These include day classes and remedial provision in ordinary schools; observation and treatment centres attached to school psychological, child guidance and child psychiatric centres; special hostels; residential homes and schools of various kinds. Where removal from his own home becomes necessary, care is needed to ensure that the 'cure' is not worse than the 'disease'—the most highly skilled substitute care is needed if the damaged child is to be rehabilitated. This means that loving care by itself is not enough while a mainly custodial regime evades the basic issues. All residential facilities must be so staffed and organized as to be therapeutic communities if this purpose is to be achieved.

However, the continuing short-comings of all day and residential services—their fragmentation, lack of communication and co-ordination; the immense variation in provision from one authority to another; and the chronic shortage of every type of trained personnel—mean that too little is available too late for the many children in urgent need of help (Pringle, 1965). Inevitably, this applies to the illegitimately born as it does to all other children.

The cost of prevention

There are some who argue that as a society we simply cannot afford to pay for comprehensive preventive services. Though plausible at first glance, surely this is fallacious? Failure to make available such services for all children and families who require them, merely postpones the day when the community has to shoulder the consequences of its failure to support early intervention. And in the long run, the cost is extremely high: not only in terms of human misery and wasted potentialities but also in terms of unemployability, mental ill health and crime. The cost would even be higher if provision for the two latter were to become more adequate and less cheese-paring than they are at present (say in the case of mental hospitals), and not mainly custodial (as it is currently in borstals and prisons).

Even in the short run, it is by no means economic to do too little and to do it too late. Take as an example whether help is given to a child while he lives at home and attends an ordinary school; or whether, though at home, he receives treatment in a special day centre; or whether he is removed from home to a residential establishment of one kind or another.

'The cost, in round figures, of a service depends almost entirely on whether it is residential, day or ambulant in nature and very little on the type of agency or the specific content of the service. For example, children treated on a 'casework' basis, whether in the probation service or child psychiatry, cost around £50 a year. Children receiving day care cost about £200 a year—whether at a day centre or an ESN school. Children who are away, whether in maladjusted schools, or in the care of children's departments, cost about £500 a year each' (Pond and Arie, 1971).

So it is evident that the lack of adequate day care and treatment—both in quantity and quality—is by no means a prudent economy, even in mere financial terms. Add to this the invisible and incalculable costs of 'parentectomy'—a term coined by a paediatrician for removing a child, particularly a young one, from his own home—and then the apparent economy of not having early, effective and professional supplementary day care and treatment provision can be seen for the self-deluding myth it is.

Future options

It may seem that we have ranged far wider than our terms of reference, namely illegitimately born children and their needs in the light of our own and other people's findings. The reason for doing so is because many, if not most, of their needs seem to be shared by other disadvantaged or underprivileged children. Also there is a danger in being too specific, losing sight of the central fact that all children share the same basic emotional, social and educational needs. In the past this has happened in relation to services for handicapped children to their detriment (Younghusband, Birchall, Davie and Pringle, 1970).

Indeed, singling out a specific condition, especially one so highly emotionally charged by social conventions and prejudice as illegitimacy, may delay dealing with its consequences in a comprehensive and compassionate way. 'In a statistical sense the unwed mother and the illegitimate baby are deviants ... Just how deviant in a social sense the unwed mother is considered is a matter about which we have many conflicting opinions, numerous stereotypes, and infinitesimal amount of data ... Undue preoccupation with illegitimacy can, however, retard the alleviation of the problems of the individual mother and child' (Giovannoni, 1970). Though these views on illegitimacy are based on experience in the United States, they apply with equal force in this country.

This, then, is the first option: whether to have comprehensive services which focus on the needs of the whole child rather than on the specific nature of his particular type of deviancy, handicap or problem.

The second option relates to research: at present our knowledge of child development, family dynamics, the interaction of economic, social and personal factors—indeed, most of the major questions regarding normal and deviant behaviour among both children and adults require further study, both theoretical and applied; partly due to lack of knowledge, our methods of detection, assessment and intervention are still crude.

There are some who argue that it is unethical to carry out the necessary research to improve available tools and techniques for prediction and prevention. But surely the opposite is the case, provided all appropriate safeguards are adopted, such as the preservation of anonymity and the avoidance of measures known to be harmful. 'It is unethical not to submit specific therapies to the experimental approach ... If the welfare society has a duty to help the deprived, it also has an obligation to provide the most effective help' (Richardson, 1967).

The third option overrides the first two since everything hinges on it: this is the question of national priorities. How much of our national resources are we prepared to spend on a comprehensive preventive service and on the necessary research to make it fully effective? At present it has the lowest possible priority. For example, central government allocates over 50 per cent of its research budget to aviation alone and a fraction of one per cent to research into respectively child development or education or the social sciences. In industry it is taken for granted that a percentage of the profits must be allocated to research and development. In consequence, more is annually spent on research into glue or whitewash than into child care.

If a reconsideration of our national priorities leads to a shift in the direction of putting human needs higher than they are at present, then four things must be done: to take stock of past research, and here a beginning has been made in some areas (Dinnage and Pringle, 1967a and 1967b; Dinnage, 1970; Pringle, 1966); to apply now what is known already; to mount a series of longitudinal and long-term inquiries; and to set in train development work so that experimental schemes can be monitored and evaluated. Only in this way can preventive work become attuned to the needs of children as well as to changing social and economic conditions.

A multi-disciplinary approach must be adopted with the emphasis shifted to the earliest stages of a child's development; with information and counselling services being readily available; and with preventive planning pushed back very much earlier—for optimal effectiveness to conception or before.

Eventually, it may well be possible to show that 'wantedness' is the most important factor in giving a baby the best long-term chance in life; it may turn out to be an even more potent variable than social class or methods of child rearing. Be this as it may, there is little doubt that the incidence of maladjustment, backwardness and delinquency would be significantly reduced here and now, if the slogan 'every child a wanted child' became a reality. Technically this is almost possible now in advanced countries. Appropriate moral and social education of tomorrow's parents could hasten the day when society really cares for the child it chooses to have.

APPENDIX

A note on the tables

This appendix includes a number of the important tables referred to in the report, together with the results of statistical tests and other notes for those tables which appear in condensed form in the main body of the report.

The appendix tables have been numbered to correspond with the chapters where reference is made to them. They are usually percentaged on column totals, excluding any 'no information' category. The results of any statistical tests performed are shown below them.

It should be noted that total populations often vary from one table to another; it has been our consistent policy to include children with only partial information in any table in which it is possible to do this correctly.

I   STATISTICS AND SAMPLE *by A. P. Round*

   1. Statistics and Data Processing
   2. Description of the Sample and its Identification

II   NOTES AND STATISTICAL TESTS FOR THE MAIN TEXT TABLES

III   TABLES NOT INCLUDED IN THE TEXT

APPENDIX I
Statistics and Sample
by A. P. Round

1. Statistics and data processing

A LARGE NUMBER of the variables which have been investigated are of a qualitative nature, and the contingency table has been a natural way of investigating possible associations between them. The overall chi-square test is then an appropriate test of the null hypothesis that no association exists.

For a number of 2 x k contingency tables (the dichotomous variable commonly being legitimate/all illegitimate) a natural ordering exists in the k-valued variable and a test for a linear trend in the proportion of illegitimates, say, in the k groups has been made using integers 1 to k as scores. In a few cases a component of the overall chi-square for quadratic trend has also been isolated (Bhapkar, 1968).

For some 2 x 2 contingency tables, with small numbers in certain cells, recourse to Fisher's exact test has been made.

A number of ordered variables are of course quantitative, but lack of time has prevented, in general, a more complex analysis. However, in a few cases where the average value of a quantitative variable (e.g. birthweight, or a test score) is of interest it has been possible to perform an analysis of variance, using multiple regression techniques since the data inevitably form a non-orthogonal or unbalanced design with a number of covariables. In this way we have attempted to isolate the effects of particular factors on an outcome variable, using an additive main effects model. Contrasts between extreme groups for the different factors in these analyses have been illustrated so that they can be compared with one another.

Since the residual mean square is calculated with a large number of degrees of freedom, chi-square rather than F values have been quoted as tests of significance of the effects of different factors. The dependent variables reading score and arithmetic score were transformed using an inverse sine transformation, and the Bristol Social-Adjustment Guide score using a square root transformation, in an attempt to stabilize their variance.

The limitations of this method of analysis should be borne in mind—the assumption of additivity is a strong one, and the diagrams may not clearly indicate the relative error with which certain constants have been estimated. For technical reasons it was unfortunately not possible to test for interactive effects in a few cases where they might have been of interest, e.g. between mother working and legitimacy status, or parental interest and legitimacy status, on attainment outcomes.

The following abbreviations have been used in various places in the report:

ns	not significant, $p > \cdot 05$
*	$\cdot 01 < p < \cdot 05$
**	$\cdot 001 < p < \cdot 01$
***	$p < \cdot 001$
df	degrees of freedom.

Some initial tables were produced from counter-sorter runs, but the majority of tables, and all the analyses, were produced using computer programs to which the Institute of Child Health (University of London), and the National Children's Bureau have contributed. The original version of the tabulation programme was made available by the Office of Population Censuses and Surveys, Social Survey division. The computers at Imperial College and the University of London Computer Centre have been used.

A lengthier discussion of the data processing is contained in *From Birth to Seven* (Davie, Butler and Goldstein, 1971).

2. Description of the sample and its identification

As the whole cohort has been adequately described elsewhere (Davie *et al.*, 1971), this discussion is confined to the way in which the illegitimate sample was identified, and any biases which may have arisen as a result of this method of identification.

Children were identified as illegitimate in the following ways:

1. If they were included in the Perinatal Mortality Survey (1958); their mothers had given their marital status as single, widowed, separated, or divorced, or stated they were cohabiting; and a subsequent registration indicated that the child was illegitimate.

2. If they were included in the National Child Development Study (1965); information available then suggested that they might have been born illegitimate, and their birth registration confirmed this.

It was estimated from General Register Office data that approximately 828 illegitimate maternities occurred in the study week (95 per cent confidence limits are 772 and 884); percentage in Table 2.1 and Table A2.1 use this estimated figure.

The study identified 673 illegitimate maternities (6 of twins) and all other maternities were classed as legitimate. Evidence from other studies conducted at about the same time (GRO 1961, Aberdeen 1961–4) suggests that the proportion of single women identified is fairly representative, and that the majority of untraced women would have been married and cohabiting.

A primary potential source of bias, then, is the fact that a number of illegitimate children were not so identified. Since the Perinatal Mortality Survey included some 98 per cent of births in the study week it is clear that a number of such children have been included in the legitimate sample.

Apart from the possible marital status bias mentioned above, it is of interest to know whether or not any social class bias has occurred in this identification procedure. Unfortunately no external data have been found with which such a comparison could be made. Comparisons were made, however, between the identified illegitimate and legitimate samples on mother's father's social class (1958), as was mentioned in Chapter 4, and they were shown to have similar distributions (including similar proportions with no information). As those with 'no information' on this measure in the identified illegitimate sample are apparently (from mother's occupation information) principally drawn from social classes IV and V, as are the 'no information' group in the whole cohort (Butler and Bonham, 1963) it seems likely that no strong biases exist.

As for the 1965 social class measure, it would be rather speculative to comment on its distribution within the unidentified illegitimate children. We can, however, comment on the biases due to those children without 1965 data. No evidence has been found of a differing pattern of information loss by social class in the identified illegitimate and legitimate samples; though a higher proportion of the illegitimate sample did not have 1965 data.

APPENDIX II
Notes and Statistical tests for the main text tables

Table 5.1   *Week of first ante-natal care visit*, for illegitimate (N = 657), legitimate less pre-marital conceptions (N — 15,533), and pre-marital conceptions (N = 804).
Tests:
Illegitimate/all legitimate, by no ante-natal care/the rest.
   Chi-square = 586·05 (1 df), $p < ·001$ (Also significant for first-borns only).
Pre-marital conceptions/legitimate first-borns, by no ante-natal care/the rest.
   Chi-square = 7·01 (1 df), $p < ·01$
All legitimate/illegitimate, by date of first visit for ante-natal care.
   Chi-square (overall) = 611·21 (5 df), $p < ·001$
   Chi-square (trend) = 139·66 (1 df), $p < ·001$ (Also significant for first-borns only).
Pre-marital conceptions/legitimate first-borns, by date of first visit for ante-natal care.
   Chi-square (overall) = 522·14 (5 df), $p < ·001$
   Chi-square (trend) = 470·94 (1 df), $p < ·001$
Pre-marital conceptions/illegitimate first-borns, by date of first visit for ante-natal care.
   Chi-square (overall) = 67·54 (5 df), $p < ·001$
   Chi-square (trend) = 38·98 (1 df), $p < ·001$

Table 5.2   *Planning for the confinement*, for illegitimate (N — 657), legitimate less pre-marital conceptions (N = 15,533), and pre-marital conceptions (N = 804).
Tests:
All legitimate/illegitimate, by booked/unbooked.
   Chi-square = 377·00 (1 df), $p < ·001$
Pre-marital conceptions/other legitimates, by booked/unbooked.
   Chi-square = 12·56 (1 df), $p < ·001$

Table 5.3   *Place of delivery*, for illegitimate (N = 657), legitimate less pre-marital conceptions (N = 15,533), and pre-marital conceptions (N = 804).
Tests:
All legitimate/illegitimate, by emergency hospital admissions as a proportion of those not booked for hospital.
   Chi-square = 26·03 (1 df), $p < ·001$

Table 6.1 *Percentage distribution of birthweight,* for all legitimate (N = 16,337) and illegitimate (N = 657).
Tests:
All legitimate/illegitimate, by 500 gramme groups.
Chi-square (overall) = 55·5 (7 df), p < ·001
Chi-square (trend) = 50·6 (1 df), p < ·001

Table 6.2 *Percentage distribution of length of gestation,* for all legitimate (N = 16,337), and illegitimate (N = 657).
Tests:
All legitimate/illegitimate, by length of gestation in weeks (grouped).
Chi-square (overall) = 19·58 (4 df), p < ·001
Chi-square (second-order trend) = 9·97 (1 df), p < ·01
All legitimate/illegitimate, by known /not known length of gestation,
Chi-square = 131·09 (1 df), p < ·001

Table 6.3 *Birthweight for gestation,* (where known), for all legitimate (N = 13,988), and illegitimate (N = 463).
Tests:
All legitimate/illegitimate, by birthweight for gestation in percentile groups.
Chi-square (overall) = 15·34 (5 df), p < ·01
Chi-square (trend) = 11·40 (1 df), p < ·001

Table 7.1 *Mortality, still-births and neonatal deaths,*[1] for the illegitimate (deaths = 34, N = 657), legitimate less pre-marital conceptions (deaths = 554, N = 15,533), and pre-marital conceptions (deaths = 29, N = 804).
[1] Neonatal deaths are those occurring within the first 4 weeks after birth.
Tests:
Legitimate/illegitimate, by deaths/survivors.
Chi-square = 3·84 (1 df), p < ·05

Table 8.1 *Family situation of the seven-year-olds,* for all illegitimate, including the adopted (N = 547)—illegitimate (N = 366), adopted (N = 181) and legitimate (N = 14,949).
Note: This table includes 21 adopted children who did not subsequently participate in the study but whom we know to have been adopted by other than their own mothers. Those illegitimates with no parental information (22) are the four per cent with no data.

Table 8.2 *Number of illegitimately born children who live in the different family situations at the age of seven.* (N = 504 i.e. all those with data on their parental situation who participated in the study).

Table 8.3 *Family situation of seven-year-olds related to mother's marital status at the time of birth,* for unsupported single (N = 441), once-married (N = 90), supported single (N = 69), and once-married cohabiting (N = 66). In six cases the status was not known in sufficient detail, but four of these were cohabiting, and were with their natural parents in 1965.

Table 8.4 *Paternal occupational status of the seven-year-olds,* for illegitimate not adopted (N = 366), illegitimate adopted (N = 160), and legitimate (N = 14,949).
Tests:

Legitimate/illegitimate not adopted, by paternal occupation groups.
Chi-square (overall) = 44·84 (4 df), p < ·001
Chi-square (trend) = 43·29 (1 df), p < ·001
Legitimate/illegitimate adopted, by paternal occupation groups.
Chi-square (overall) = 34·56 (4 df), p < ·001
Chi-square (trend) = 25·64 (1 df), p < ·001
Chi-square (departure) = 8·92 (1 df), p < ·05

Chapter 8 *Relinquishing child for adoption within social class of upbringing of mother.* Adopted/not adopted, by three social class groups.
Chi-square (trend) = 4·06 (1 df), p < ·05

Table 8.5 *Mother worked before child went to school,* for illegitimate not adopted (N = 316), illegitimate adopted (N = 141), and legitimate (N = 13,535) i.e. all those with information, on the parental questionnaire.
Tests:

Legitimate/illegitimate not adopted, by mother working before child goes to school (part-time/full-time/not).
Chi-square = 452·42 (2 df), p < ·001
Legitimate/illegitimate adopted, by mother working before child goes to school (part-time/full-time/not).
Chi-square = 19·95 (2 df), p < ·001

Table 8.6 *Mother worked after child went to school,* for illegitimate not adopted (N = 317), illegitimate adopted (N = 147), and legitimate (N = 13,890).
Tests:

Legitimate/illegitimate not adopted, by mother working after child goes to school (part-time/full-time/not).
Chi-square = 118·19 (2 df), p < ·001
Legitimate/illegitimate adopted, by mother working after child goes to school (part-time/full-time/not).
Chi-square = 6·74 (2 df), p < ·05

Figure 8.1 *Family size in 1965, see Table A8.5.*

Chapter 9   *Death before seven years:*
Legitimate/all illegitimate, by deaths from 4 weeks to 7 years/ survivors.
      Chi-square = 5·45 (1 df), p < ·02

Chapter 9   *Accidents:*
Although tested, the findings on accidents for children living with their own mother only, were not statistically proven. The subject has been mentioned as being worthy of further investigation.

Chapter 9   *Growth:*
Illegitimate not adopted/illegitimate adopted, by tall children/the rest.
      Chi-square = 7·52 (2 df), p < ·05

Chapter 9   *Vision and hearing*
Tests for legitimate/illegitimate not adopted, and for legitimate/ illegitimate adopted, were not significant. Legitimate/all illegitimate, by vision and by hearing were not significant either.

Chapter 9   *Speech:*
Legitimate/illegitimate not adopted, by speech intelligibility.
      Chi-square = 4·47 (1 df), p < ·05

Table 9.1   *Teacher's assessment of clumsiness,* for all illegitimate (N = 486), and legitimate (N = 14,418).
Tests:
Legitimate/all illegitimate, by clumsiness (not applicable/somewhat/ certainly).
      Chi-square (overall) = 11·63 (2 df), p < ·01
      Chi-square (trend) = 11·6 (1 df), p < ·001

Table 9.2   *Teacher's assessment of restless behaviour,* for all illegitimate (N = 489), and legitimate (N = 14,457).
Tests:
Legitimate/all illegitimate, by restlessness (not applicable/some-what/certainly).
      Chi-square (overall) = 13·78 (2 df), p < .01
      Chi-square (trend) = 12·48 (1 df), p < ·001

Table 9.3   *Attendance at child health clinic up to the age of one year,* for illegitimate not adopted (N = 334), illegitimate adopted (N = 140), and legitimate (N = 14,167). Only those with a known social class were used for this analysis.
Tests:
Legitimate/illegitimate, by attendance (regularly/occasionally/not at all).
      Chi-square (overall) = 27·33 (2 df), p < ·001
      Chi-square (trend) = 25·21 (1 df), p < ·001

Illegitimate not adopted/illegitimate adopted, by attendance (regularly/occasionally/not at all).
Chi-square (overall) = 29·91 (2 df), p < ·001
Chi-square (trend) = 23·87 (1 df), p < ·001

Chapter 10 *Teacher's assessment of need of special education:*
Legitimate/illegitimate not adopted, by would not benefit from special schooling/would benefit.
Chi-square = 20·38 (1 df), p < ·001

Table 11.1 *Bristol Social-Adjustment Guide Scores,* for illegitimate not adopted (N = 344) illegitimate adopted (N = 146), and legitimate (N = 14,417).
Tests:
Legitimate/illegitimate not adopted, by grouped BSAG score distribution (0–4/5–9/ etc.).
Chi-square (overall) = 55·97 (5 df), p < ·001
Chi-square (trend) = 53·38 (1 df), p < ·001
Legitimate/illegitimate adopted, by grouped BSAG score distribution (0–4/5–9/etc.).
Chi-square (overall) = 2·03 (5 df), ns
Chi-square (trend) = 0·28 (1 df), ns

Table 11.2 *School attendance and parental condoning of absence,* for illegitimate not adopted (N = 339), illegitimate adopted (N = 140), and legitimate (N = 14,371).
Tests:
Legitimate/illegitimate not adopted, by school attendance (90 per cent/76–89 per cent/under 75 per cent).
Chi-square (overall) = 21·82 (2 df), p < ·001
Chi-square (trend) = 18·19 (1 df), p < ·001
Legitimate/illegitimate adopted, by school attendance (90 per cent/76–89 per cent/under 75 per cent).
Chi-square (overall) = 1·24 (2 df), ns
Chi-square (trend) = 1·13 (1 df), ns
Legitimate/illegitimate not adopted, by parental condoning(yes/no).
Chi-square = 11·46 (1 df), p < ·001

Figures   *Note:* Differences in distribution between illegitimate and legitimate
11.1 and   were in all cases significant. Differences between legitimate and the
11.2   adopted illegitimate were significant only in I, II, and III NM, and not within sex groupings. (Tables and chi-squares available).

Chapter 11 Two parents/own mother and no male head, by grouped BSA6 score
page 88   (0–9/10–19/20 +).
Chi-square (overall) = 8·31 (2 df), p < ·02
Chi-square (trend) = 12·60 (1 df), p < ·01

Chapter 11 Legitimate/illegitimate not adopted, by attendance at child guidance
page 90   clinic.
Chi-square = 10·12 (1 df), p < ·001

APPENDIX III

Tables not Included in the Text

TABLE A2.1: *Evidence on the extent of cohabitation amongst mothers having illegitimate children taken from British research*[1]

INFORMATION ON COHABITATION	1949 LEICESTER		1958 PERINATAL MORTALITY SURVEY†		1961–64 ABERDEEN		1961 GRO	
	N	%	N	%	N	%	N	%
Single cohabiting	45	32	71	14	52	11	89	16
Single not cohabiting	96	68	438	86	413	89	464	84
Total single	141	100	509	100	465	100	553	100
Once-married cohabiting	75	75	69	44	126	54	201	62
Once-married not cohabiting	24	25	89	56	108	46	121	38
Total once-married group	99	100	158	100	234	100	322	100
Total cohabiting	120	42	144‡	17	178	25	290	27
Total not cohabiting	120	42	527	64	521	75	585	55
Registration not known or missing from sample	44	16	157	19	0	0	184	17

[1]The total cohabiting has been percentaged out of a total which includes the 'not known' registrations, since these could not be assigned to any group. The single and once-married are percentaged on the known registrations for each group respectively.

†Figures for the PMS are based on the estimated maternities resulting in illegitimate birth registrations for one week in March 1958 for England, Wales and Scotland, according to the nearest available figures from the GRO.

‡The sum of the total single and once-married registrations gives four less than for all cohabitations. This is due to the fact that on four schedules the status was not known but the mother was known to be cohabiting.

NB Percentages have been rounded.

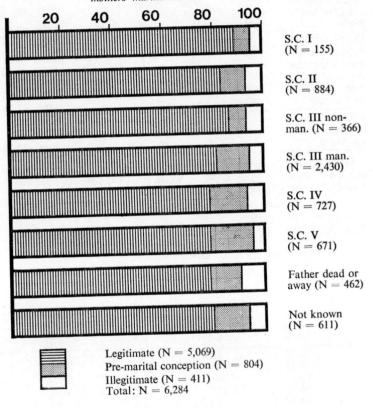

FIGURE A4.1: *First births by mothers' fathers' social class and mothers' marital status*

Legitimate (N = 5,069)
Pre-marital conception (N = 804)
Illegitimate (N = 411)
Total: N = 6,284

TABLE A5.1: *The excess risk of infant mortality of illegitimate over legitimate and changes in the illegitimate infant mortality rates between 1958–66*[1]

| | 1958 | | 1966 | | EXCESS OF ILLEGITIMATE *Rate over Legitimate Rate as % of Legitimate Rate* | |
	ILLEGIT-IMATE	LEGIT-IMATE	ILLEGIT-IMATE	LEGIT-IMATE		
Infant mortality per 1,000 live births (4 wks–1 year)	7·2	6·4	6·7	6·1	1958 1966	12·50 9·85
Stillbirth rates per 1,000 births Neonatal death rate (0–4 weeks)	28·4 20·6	21·2 15·9	18·6 17·8	15·1 12·4	1958 1966 1958 1966	34·31 23·16 29·56 43·55
Stillbirth and neonatal deaths combined	49·0	37·0	36·4	27·5	1958 1966	32·4 32·22

[1]The figures for infant mortality and neonatal death are taken from the Annual Reports of the Chief Medical Officer, whilst those for stillbirth rates may be found in the GRO Statistical Review (1966) Tables C1 and C1 Part II.

TABLE A5.2: *Week of first ante-natal visit. All illegitimate by marital status groups*

| WEEK OF FIRST VISIT | UNSUPPORTED | | ALL COHABITATIONS |
	Single Not Cohabiting	*Ever-Married not Cohabiting*	
No pre-natal visits	%	%	%
	8·3	8·3	5·1
1– 7	1·1	3·6	6·5
8–15	18·4	16·7	15·2
16–23	20·9	20·2	31·1
24–31	31·5	32·1	24·6
32–35	7·6	8·3	7·2
36 or later	6·7	3·6	3·6
NK	5·5	7·1	6·5
Total	100·0 (435)	100·0 (84)	100·0 (138)

All unsupported/cohabiting.
  Chi-square = 18·70 (5 df), p < ·01

TABLE A5.3: *Distribution of mother's haemoglobin level for legitimate, illegitimate and pre-marital conceptions*

LEVEL OF HAEMOGLOBIN	ILLEGITIMATE	LEGITMATE	PRE-MARITAL CONCEPTION
Under 60%	4·0	2·5	2·2
60–69%	15·2	11·7	12·4
70% or over	80·8	85·8	85·5
Total tested	100·0 (422)	100·0 (9962)	100·0 (599)
Not tested	30·9	32·8	21·6
No information	4·9	3·1	3·9
Total including no information	100·0 (657)	100·0 (15533)	100·0 (804)

All legitimate (including pre-marital conceptions)/illegitimate.
Chi-square (overall) = 8·81 (2 df), p < ·02
Chi-square (trend) = 8·8 (1 df), p < ·01

APPENDIX ANALYSIS 6.1: *Analysis of birthweight*
Main effects model
Dependent variable is birthweight (gms)
Idependent variables are as shown below.
  Sample size = 14449
  Mean birthweight = 3308·24 gms

Fitted Constants and Analysis of Variance table
x^2 values are adjusted for the other factors

Source		Fitted Constant	DF	χ^2	
Overall		3219·9			
Mother's Age:	19 or less	— 7·4	2	6·18	*
	20–29	16·8			
	30 +	— 9·4			
Parity:	0	—116·5	3	175·50	***
	1	6·3			
	2 + 3	31·0			
	4 +	75·2			
Mother's Height coeff. (increase, gms per inch, measured about 63·5 inches) (1 inch = 2·54 cms)		39·5	1	427·97	***
Legitimacy:	Legitimate	21·1	1	1·82	ns
	Illegitimate	— 21·1			
Smoking in Pregnancy:					
	Non-smoker	83·0	1	266·69	***
	Smoker	— 83·0			
Toxaemia:	None	75·1	3	155·28	***
	Mild or moderate	98·1			
	Severe	—147·0			
	Remainder	— 26·2			
Sex:	Boy	65·9	1	191·66	***
	Girl	— 65·9			
Mother's Father's Social Class:					
	I, II, III non-manual	20·6	4	9·32	ns
	III manual	14·7			
	IV	— 19·9			
	V	— 6·9			
	All other except 'don't know'	— 8·5			
For Illegitimates:					
	Cohabiting	63·6	1	4·24	*
	Not cohabiting	— 63·6			

Residual mean square = 326163·89

Total variance = 355753·30

Combining the Legitimacy/Illegitimacy and Cohabiting/not Cohabiting factors we have:

	Legitimate	21·1
	Illegitimate Cohabiting	42·4
	Illegitimate not Cohabiting	— 84·7

TABLE A7.1: *Maternal age of illegitimate, legitimate and pre-marital conception population (P), and deaths (D) with incidence of death in each cell*

MATERNAL AGE		ILLEGITIMATE		ALL LEGITIMATE		PRE-MARITAL CONCEPTION	
		N	%	N	%	N	%
Under 20 years	P	164	(25·0)	814	(5·0)	374	(46·5)
	D	7	4·3	19	2·3	13	3·5
20–24 years	P	219	(33·0)	4,710	(28·8)	354	(44·0)
	D	7	3·2	155	3·3	11	3·1
25–29 years	P	126	(19·2)	5,325	(32·6)	53	(6·6)
	D	6	4·8	169	3·2	4	7·5
30–34 years	P	86	(13·1)	3,337	(20·4)	15	(1·9)
	D	8	9·3	129	3·9	1	6·7
35–39 years	P	48	(7·3)	1,705	(10·4)	6	(0·6)
	D	6	12·5	75	4·4	0	0·0
40 + years	P	13	(2·0)	436	(2·7)	2	(0·0)
	D	0	0·0	34	7·8	0	0·0
No information	P	1	(0·2)	10	(0·1)	76	(9·4)
	D	0	0·0	1	10·0	5	6·6
Total	P	657	(100·0)	16,337	(100·0)	804	(100·0)
	D	34	5·2	582	3·6	29	3·6

NB

1. For this, and the following appendix table(s), the bracketed percentages are the ones which show the distribution in the sample and add up to 100 per cent. The others give the rate of deaths for each cell, e.g. 4·9 is the death rate for the illegitimate mothers having their first baby, etc.

2. Pre-marital conceptions have not been subtracted from the legitimate sample, since our main concern is with differences between the illegitimate and legitimate. Because the pre-marital conceptions were all of one parity group they were normally compared with groups of the same parity in the other two samples. These tables are available but it has not been possible to include them in this appendix.

TABLE A7.2: *Parity (birth order) for illegitimate and legitimate population (P) and deaths (D) with incidence of death, in each cell*

PARITY OF MOTHER		ILLEGITIMATE		ALL LEGITIMATE	
		N	%	N	%
0	P	411	(62·6)	5,873	(36·1)
	D	20	4·9	231	3·9
1	P	107	(16·3)	5,108	(31·3)
	D	5	4·7	136	2·7
2 & 3	P	82	(12·5)	3,895	(23·8)
	D	3	3·7	143	3·7
4 +	P	57	(8·7)	1,459	(8·9)
	D	6	10·5	72	4·9
Total including no information	P	657	(100·0)	16,337	(100·0)
	D	34	5·2	582	3·6

TABLE A7.3: *Mothers' fathers' social class of illegitimate, legitimate and pre-marital conception population (P) and deaths (D) with incidence of death in each cell*

MOTHERS' FATHERS' SOCIAL CLASS		ILLEGITIMATE		ALL LEGITIMATE		PRE-MARITAL CONCEPTION	
		N	%	N	%	N	%
I and II	P	102	(15·6)	2,525	(15·4)	94	(11·6)
	D	5	4·9	63	2·5	2	2·1
III non-manual	P	30	(4·6)	851	(5·2)	26	(3·2)
	D	2	6·7	20	2·4	1	3·8
III manual	P	217	(33·0)	6,092	(37·3)	331	(41·2)
	D	8	3·7	214	3·5	11	3·3
IV	P	93	(14·2)	2,025	(12·4)	109	(13·6)
	D	7	7·5	84	4·1	4	3·7
V	P	84	(12·8)	1,887	(11·6)	101	(12·6)
	D	3	3·6	77	4·1	3	3·0
Miscellaneous or DK	P	131	(19·9)	2,957	(18·1)	143	(17·7)
	D	9	6·9	124	4·2	8	5·6
Total	P	657	(100·0)	16,337	(100·0)	804	(100·0)
	D	34	5·2	582	3·6	29	3·6

TABLE A7.4: *Maternal height, grouped into tall, short and medium categories, for legitimate, illegitimate and pre-marital conception population (P) and deaths (D), with death incidence in each cell*

HEIGHT IN INCHES		ILLEGITIMATE		LEGITIMATE		PRE-MARITAL CONCEPTION	
		N	%	N	%	N	%
Under 62"	P	144	21·9	3450	21·1	182	22·6
	D	8	5·6	153	4·4	10	5·5
62"–64"	P	297	45·2	7530	46·1	361	44·9
	D	15	5·1	227	3·0	10	2·8
65" +	P	176	26·8	4708	28·8	227	28·2
	D	8	4·5	136	2·9	6	2·6
NK	P	40	6·1	649	4·0	34	4·2
	D	3	7·5	66	10·2	3	8·8
Total	P	657	100·0	16,337	100·0	804	100·0
	D	34	5·2	582	3·6	29	3·6

Legitimate/illegitimate population.
Chi-square (overall) = 0·92 (2 df), ns
Chi-square (trend) = 0·92 (1 df), ns

TABLE A7.5: *Toxaemia for illegitimate, legitimate and pre-marital conceptions population (P) and deaths (D) with death incidence in each cell*

Toxaemia Group		Illegitimate		Legitimate		Pre-Marital Conception	
		N	%	N	%	N	%
None	P	385	(58·6)	10,611	(65·0)	512	(63·7)
	D	9	2·3	283	2·7	10	2·0
Mild	P	97	(14·8)	2857	(17·5)	124	(15·4)
	D	8	8·2	91	3·2	5	4·0
Moderate	P	19	(2·9)	659	(4·0)	28	(3·5)
	D	0	0·0	20	3·0	1	3·6
Severe	P	52	(7·9)	986	(6·0)	52	(6·5)
	D	3	5·8	99	10·0	6	11·5
Remainder Proteinuria, unclassified and insufficient information	P	104	(15·8)	1224	(7·5)	88	(10·9)
	D	14	13·5	89	7·3	7	8·0
Total	P	657	(100·0)	16,337	(100·0)	804	(100·0)
	D	34		582		29	

Legitimate/illegitimate population, by unclassified remainder/other groups.
    Chi-square = 59·79 (1 df), p < ·001
Illegitimate (deaths/survivors), by Unclassified remainder/other groups.
    Chi-square = 15·34 (1 df), p < ·001

TABLE A7.6: *Smoking for illegitimate, legitimate and pre-marital conception population (P) and deaths (D) with incidence of death in each cell*

SMOKING		ILLEGITIMATE		ALL LEGITIMATE		PRE-MARITAL CONCEPTION	
		N	%	N	%	N	%
Non-smoker	P	375	(57·1)	10,770	(65·9)	519	(64·6)
	D	17	4·5	344	3·2	24	4·6
Smoker	P	208	(31·6)	4452	(27·5)	215	(26·7)
	D	15	7·2	193	4·3	3	1·4
DK/or variable	P	74	(11·2)	1115	(6·8)	70	(8·7)
	D	2	2·7	45	4·0	2	2·8
Total	P	657	(100·0)	16,337	(100·0)	804	(100·0)
	D	34	5·2	582	3·6	29	3·6

Legitimate/illegitimate population, by non-smokers/smokers.
Chi-square = 10·86 (1 df), p < ·001

TABLE A7.7: *Birthweight, with incidence of death for illegitimate and legitimate*

BIRTHWEIGHT GROUPS		ILLEGITIMATE		ALL LEGITIMATE	
		N	%	N	%
< 1001	P	3	(0·5)	47	(0·3)
	D	3	100·0	47	100·0
1001–1500	P	9	(1·4)	91	(0·6)
	D	7	77·8	76	83·5
1501–2000	P	15	(2·3)	158	(1·0)
	D	8	53·3	70	44·3
2001–2500	P	45	(6·9)	686	(4·2)
	D	6	13·3	61	8·9
Total < 2501 (inc. est. wt)	P	74	(11·3)	1,065	(6·5)
	D	25	33·8	292	27·4
2501–3000	P	139	(21·2)	2,921	(17·9)
	D	3	2·2	100	3·4
3001–4000	P	385	(58·6)	10,304	(63·1)
	D	6	1·6	141	1·4
> 4001	P	36	(5·5)	1,550	(9·5)
	D	0	0·0	21	1·4
Total > 2500 (inc. est. wt)	P	583	(88·7)	15,203	(93·1)
	D	9	1·5	287	1·9
Total (inc. no information)	P	657	(100·0)	16,337	(100·0)
	D	34	5·2	582	3·6

TABLE A8.1: *Analysis of changes in the size and composition of the illegitimately born sample*

A. *Perinatal Mortality Survey*   N
    (single and multiple births in the week 3rd–9th March 1958)   669
    six pairs of twins were excluded only from perinatal analyses, hence
    N = 657

Unavoidable losses:	stillborn	21
	neonatal death	18
		—
		39
		—

B. *All Children from the Above Survey Surviving four Weeks After Birth*   630

Gains: illegitimate births identified		
during follow-up at seven years	10	640
Unavoidable losses:	died	11
	emigrated	11
		—
		22
		—
Avoidable losses:	refused	4
	untraced	66
		—
		70
		—
Adopted:		182

C. *Sample of Illegitimate, not Adopted Seven-year-olds*   366
    Additionally, in a number of cases it did not prove possible to obtain
    one or more completed assessment schedules. Their numbers were as
    follows:

    22 parental interviews
    21 educational assessments
    47 medical assessments

D. *Sample of Illegitimate Adopted Seven-year-olds* (N = 182 – 22)   160

Unavoidable losses:	died	1
	emigrated	5
		—
		6
		—
Avoidable losses:	refused	5
	untraced	11
		—
		16
		—

TABLE A8.2: *Occupational status by family situation for the non-adopted illegitimate seven-year-olds*

1965 SOCIAL CLASS	TWO PARENTS		OWN MOTHER		NEITHER PARENT
	Both Natural	One Natural, (Mostly Mother)	and Others	Only	
	%	%	%	%	%
I, II, III non-manual	14·4	12·3	13·2	10·0	10·8
III manual	49·3	52·1	15·8	26·0	18·9
IV and V	35·6	34·2	36·8	32·0	35·1
No data	0·7	1·4	34·2	32·0	35·1
Total	100·0	100·0	100·0	100·0	100·0
	(146)	(73)	(38)	(50)	(37)

TABLE A8.3: *Mother worked before child went to school in relation to different family situations*

	TWO PARENTS		OWN MOTHER		NEITHER PARENT
	Both Natural	One Natural, (Mostly Mother)	and Others	Only	
	%	%	%	%	%
Not worked	50·0	16·9	48·6	22·4	52·2
Part-time	18·8	13·8	8·6	24·5	21·7
Full-time	31·2	69·2	42·8	53·1	26·1
Total with information	100·0	100·0	100·0	100·0	100·0
	(144)	(65)	(35)	(49)	(23)
No information	1·4	11·0	7·9	2·0	37·8
Total	100·0	100·0	100·0	100·0	100·0
	(146)	(73)	(38)	(50)	(37)

Both natural parents/one natural (mostly mothers), by working/not working.
  Chi-square = 19·11 (1 df), p < ·001
Both natural parents/own mother only, by working/not working.
  Chi-square = 10·22 (1 df), p < ·01

TABLE A8.4: *Mother worked after child went to school in relation to different family situations*

| | TWO PARENTS | | OWN MOTHER | | NEITHER PARENT |
	Both Natural	One Natural, (Mostly Mother)	and Others	Only	
	%	%	%	%	%
Not worked	46·8	50·0	27·8	28·6	44·0
Part-time	30·5	27·3	22·2	26·5	40·0
Full-time	22·7	22·7	50·0	44·9	16·0
Total with information	100·0 (141)	100·0 (66)	100·0 (36)	100·0 (49)	100·0 (25)
No information	3·4	9·6	5·3	2·0	32·4
Total	100·0 (146)	100·0 (73)	100·0 (38)	100·0 (50)	100·0 (37)

Both natural parents/own mother only, by working/not working.
  Chi-square = 4·24 (1 df), p < ·05
Both natural parents/own mother and others, by working/not working.
  Chi-square = 3·49 (1 df), p < ·05

TABLE A8.5: *Family size*

| NO. OF CHILDREN | ILLEGITIMATE | | LEGITIMATE |
	Not Adopted	Adopted	
	%	%	%
1	21·1	25·8	8·5
2	23·0	56·3	34·8
3	23·0	9·9	26·3
4	14·6	4·6	15·2
5	6·5	2·6	7·0
6 +	11·8	0·7	8·2
Total with information	100·0 (322)	100·0 (151)	100·0 (14,138)
No information	6·4	5·6	0·8
Total	100·0 (344)	100·0 (160)	100·0 (14,248)

Legitimate/illegitimate not adopted.
  (Chi-square (overall) = 76·59 (5 df), p < ·001
  Chi-square (second order trend) = 38·23 (1 df), p < ·001
Legitimate/illegitimate adopted.
  Chi-square (overall) = 112·66 (5 df), p < ·001
  Chi-square (trend) = 77·53 (1 df), p < ·001

TABLE A8.6: *Family size in relation to different family situations*

| No. of Children | Two Parents | | Own Mother | | Neither Parent |
	Both Natural	One Natural, (Mostly Mother)	and Others	Only	
	%	%	%	%	%
1	11·0	9·0	40·5	38·8	52·2
2 or 3	45·2	65·6	40·5	26·5	43·5
4	15·1	14·9	10·8	20·4	4·3
5	11·0	4·5	0·0	4·1	0·0
6 +	17·8	6·0	8·1	10·2	0·0
Total with information	100·0 (146)	100·0 (67)	100·0 (37)	100·0 (49)	100·0 (23)
No information	0·0	8·2	2·6	2·0	37·8
Total	100·0 (146)	100·0 (73)	100·0 (38)	100·0 (50)	100·0 (37)

Both natural parents/other two-parent families, by family size (1/2 or 3/4/5 +).
  Chi-square (overall) = 10·60 (3 df), p < ·02
  Chi-square (second order trend) = 4·35 (1 df), p < ·05
  Chi-square (first order trend) = 6·06 (1 df), p < ·02

TABLE A8.7: *Moving house*

No. of Moves	Illegitimate (Not Adopted)	Legitimate
	%	%
None or 1	50·2	73·1
2–3	31·3	20·2
4–5	14·7	4·5
6 +	3·8	2·3
Total with† information	100·0 (313)	100·0 (14,064)
No information	9·0	1·3
Total	100·0 (344)	100·0 (14,248)

†Only children with a known social class were used for this analysis.
Legitimate/illegitimate not adopted, by number of moves (4 groups).
  Chi-square (overall) = 107·23 (3 df), p < ·001
  Chi-square (trend) = 81·39 (1 df), p < ·001
Legitimate/illegitimate not adopted, by number of moves (4 +/the others).
  Chi-square = 63·87 (1 df), p < ·001

TABLE A8.8: *Moving house in relation to different family situations*

No. of Moves	Two Parents		Own Mother		Neither Parent
	Both Natural	*One Natural, (Mostly Mother)*	*and Others*	*Only*	
	%	%	%	%	%
None or 1	50·7	17·2	70·3	68·7	70·0
2 or 3	31·2	45·3	27·0	20·8	20·0
4 or more	18·1	37·5	2·7	10·4	10·0
Total with information	100·0 (144)	100·0 (64)	100·0 (37)	100·0 (48)	100·0 (20)
No information	1·4	12·3	2·6	4·0	4·6
Total	100·0 (146)	100·0 (73)	100·0 (38)	100·0 (50)	100·0 (37)

Both natural parents/other two parent families.
  Chi-square (overall) = $21·74$ (2 df), $p < ·001$
  Chi-square (trend) = $20·12$ (1 df), $p < ·001$
Two parent families/others.
  Chi-square (overall) = $25·57$ (2 df), $p < ·001$
  Chi-square (trend) = 24.68 (1 df), $p < ·001$

TABLE A8.9: *Overcrowding*

Persons Per Room	Illegitimate		Legitimate
	Not Adopted	*Adopted*	
	%	%	%
Up to 1·5	78·2	94·6	85·4
1·6 + 'over-crowded'	21·8	5·3	14·6
Total with information	100·0 (303)	100·0 (131)	100·0 (13,550)
No information	12·2	18·1	4·7
Total	100·0 (344)	100·0 (160)	100·0 (14,248)

Legitimate/illegitimate not adopted.
  Chi-square = $11·57$ (1 df), $p < ·001$

TABLE A8.10: *Overcrowding in relation to family situation*

| PERSONS PER ROOM | TWO PARENTS | | OWN MOTHER | | NEITHER PARENT |
	Both Natural	*One Natural, (Mostly Mother)*	*and Others*	*Only*	
	%	%	%	%	%
Up to 1·5	70·1	85·5	84·8	81·8	86·6
1·6 + 'overcrowded'	29·9	14·5	15·2	18·2	13·3
Total with information	100·0 (134)	100·0 (62)	100·0 (33)	100·0 (44)	100·0 (30)
No information	8·2	15·1	13·1	12·0	18·9
Total	100·0 (146)	100·0 (73)	100·0 (38)	100·0 (50)	100·0 (37)

Both natural parents/the others, by overcrowding ($\leqslant 1.0$, $\leqslant 1.5$, $\leqslant 2.0$, < 2.0).
  Chi-square (overall) = 10·59 (3 df), $p < ·05$
  Chi-square (trend) = 9·65 (1 df), $p < ·01$

TABLE A8.11: *Shared or sole use of four basic amenities*

| USE OF AMENITIES | ILLEGITIMATE | | LEGITIMATE |
	Not Adopted	*Adopted*	
	%	%	%
All 4	67·0	95·2	83·5
3	10·0	2·7	6·9
2	6·5	1·4	4·5
1 only	16·5	0·7	5·1
Total with information	100·0 (321)	100·0 (145)	100·0 (13,953)
No information	6·7	9·4	1·2
Total	100·0 (344)	100·0 (160)	100·0 (14,248)

Legitimate/illegitimate not adopted.
  Chi-square (overall) = 94·34 (3 df), $p < ·001$
  Chi-square (trend) = 85·76 (1 df), $p < ·001$
Legitimate/illegitimate adopted.
  Chi-square (overall) = 14·50 (3 df), $p < ·01$
  Chi-square (trend) = 13·13 (1 df), $p < ·001$

TABLE A8.12: *Shared or sole use of four basic amenities in relation to different family situations*

USE OF AMENITIES	TWO PARENTS		OWN MOTHER		NEITHER PARENT
	Both Natural	*One Natural, (Mostly Mother)*	*and Other*	*Only*	
	%	%	%	%	%
All 4	64·5	65·6	75·0	68·7	68·8
3	12·1	7·8	8·3	6·2	12·5
2	4·3	10·9	2·8	10·4	6·2
1 only	19·1	15·6	13·9	14·6	12·5
Total with information	100·0	100·0	100·0	100·0	100·0
	(141)	(64)	(36)	(48)	(32)
No information	3·4	1·2	5·3	4·0	1·6
	100·0	100·0	100·0	100·0	100·0
Total	(146)	(73)	(38)	(50)	(37)

Both natural parents/own mother + (2 groups showing greatest difference).
  Chi-square (overall) = 1·42 (3 df), ns
  Chi-square (trend) = 1·06 (1 df), ns

TABLE A8.13: *Percentages with overt housing, financial or employment problems*

TYPE OF PROBLEM	ILLEGITIMATE		LEGITIMATE
	Not Adopted	Adopted	
	%	%	%
Housing	18·1	1·6	7·3
Financial	20·8	—	7·4
Employment	9·6	0·7	3·4
Total with information	100·0 (332)	100·0 (146)	100·0 (14,220)
No information	3·5	8·7	0·9
Total	100·0 (344)	100·0 (160)	100·0 (14,248)

NB These categories overlap and thus the percentages do not add up to 100. On each item the trend tested was 'yes', 'no', and 'don't know'.

Legitimate/illegitimate not adopted.
  Housing   chi-square $= 58·68$ (2 df), $p < ·001$
  chi-square (trend) $= 57·34$, $p < ·001$
  Financial   chi-square $= 91·38$ (2 df), $p < ·001$
  chi-square (trend) $= 86·39$, $p < ·001$
  Unemployment   chi-square $= 42·23$ (2 df), $p < ·001$
  chi-square (trend) $= 38·85$, $p < ·001$

Legitimate/illegitimate adopted.
  Housing   chi-square $= 8·90$ (2 df), $p < ·02$
  Unemployment   chi-square $= 5·13$ (2 df), ns
  chi-square (trend) $= 5·12$, $p < ·05$

TABLE A8.14: *Percentages with use of day and substitute care facilities*

	ILLEGITIMATE		LEGITIMATE
	Not Adopted	Adopted	
	%	%	%
Local Authority day nursery	16	1	2
Private nursery	4	8	4
In care (short term)	3	8	1
In care (long term)	8	19	1

Note: Table 8.14 is a summary table and percentages do not add up to 100.

TABLE A8.15: *Percentages with use of day and substitute care facilities in relation to family situation*

| | TWO PARENTS | | OWN MOTHER | | NEITHER PARENT |
	Both Natural	One Natural, (Mostly Mother)	and Others	Only	
	%	%	%	%	%
Local Authority day nursery	7	27	18	27	12
Private nursery	3	5	3	4	9
In care	6	7	10	1	41

Note: Table 8.15 is a summary table and percentages do not add up to 100.
All parental groups, by day care (Local Authority/private/neither).
   Chi-square = 21·89 (8 df), p < ·01
Both natural parents and mothers and others/the rest.
   Chi-square = 14·13 (2 df), p < ·001
Natural parents/legititimate, by in care/not in care.
   Chi-square = 11·22 (1 df), p < ·001

TABLE A9.1: *Illegitimate not adopted attendance at infant welfare clinic up to one year old by 1965 family situation*

| ATTENDANCE | TWO PARENTS | | OWN MOTHER | | NEITHER PARENT |
	Both Natural	One Natural, (Mostly Mother)	and Other	Only	
	%	%	%	%	%
Regular	51·4	40·3	44·4	28·6	25·0
Occasional	21·9	28·4	16·7	40·8	13·9
Not attended	26·0	29·8	38·9	28·6	44·4
Not known	0·7	1·5	0·0	2·0	16·7
Total with information	100·0 (146)	100·0 (67)	100·0 (36)	100·0 (49)	100·0 (36)
No information	0·0	8·2	5·3	2·0	2·8
Total	100·0 (146)	100·0 (73)	100·0 (38)	100·0 (50)	100·0 (37)

Both natural parents/the remainder.
   Chi-square (overall) = 7·5 (2 df), p < ·05
   Chi-square (trend) = 6·5 (1 df), p < ·02
Other two-parent families/remainder atypical.
   Chi-square = 1·36 (2 df), ns

TABLE A9.2: *Admission to hospital for accidents for legitimate and illegitimate*

ACCIDENTS		LEGITI-MATE	ILLEGITIMATE	
			Not Adopted	*Adopted*
Road	Yes	2·3 (329)	2·1 (7)	2·7 (4)
	No	(13,762)	(322)	(139)
Home	Yes	8·9 (1,256)	9·4 (31)	11·6 (17)
	No	(12,795)	(298)	(125)
Other	Yes	8·7 (1,231)	10·0 (33)	6·7 (10)
	No	(12,799)	(294)	(131)
Children who had† at least one accident		18·0 (2,543)	19·0 (61)	18·4 (26)

†as a proportion of all those with information on all measures.
Legitimate/illegitimate
   Chi-square (road) = 0·00 (1 df), ns
   Chi-square (home) = 0·45 (1 df), ns
   Chi-square (other) = 0·53 (1 df), ns
Illegitimate not adopted/illegitimate adopted.
   Fisher's exact test (road), p = 0·44
   Fisher's exact test (home), p = 0·45
   Fisher's exact test (other), p = 0·73

TABLE A9.3: *Admission to hospital by illegitimate parental situation.*

ACCIDENTS	TWO NATURAL PARENTS	OTHER TWO-PARENT FAMILIES	OWN MOTHER +OTHER	OWN MOTHER NO MALE HEAD	NEITHER PARENT
At least one accident	17·6 (25)	21·2 (14)	12·5 (4)	28·9 (13)	13·5 (5)
No accident	82·4 (117)	81·8 (52)	87·5 (28)	71·1 (32)	86·5 (32)
Total with information	100·0 (142)	100·0 (66)	100·0 (32)	100·0 (45)	100·0 (37)

Chi-square (overall) = 4·78 (4 df), ns
Two-parent families/own mother no male head, by accident/no accident.
   Chi-square = 1·84 (1 df), ns

TABLE A9.4: *Sex distribution in sample children*

| SEX | LEGITIMATE | ILLEGITIMATE | |
		Not Adopted	Adopted
Boys	51·4	43·2	58·8
Girls	48·6	56·8	41·3
Total	100·0	100·0	100·0
	(14,951)	(366)	(160)

Legitimate/illegitimate not adopted.
  Chi-square = 9·44 (1 df), p < ·01
Illegitimate not adopted/illegitimate adopted.
  Chi-square = 10·21 (1 df), p < ·01

TABLE A10.1: *Teacher's assessment of child's general knowledge level*

| TEACHER'S ASSESSMENT | ILLEGITIMATE | | LEGITIMATE |
	Not Adopted	Adopted	
	%	%	%
Exceptionally well-informed	0·9	3·4	2·9
Good background	9·5	31·5	20·1
Average	45·0	49·3	49·0
Below average rather limited	36·4	15·1	23·9
Largely ignorant of world around him	8·3	0·7	4·2
Total assessed	100·0	100·0	100·0
	(349)	(146)	(14,516)

Legitimate/illegitimate not adopted.
  Chi-square (overall) = 60·67 (4 df), p < ·001
  Chi-square (trend) = 59·12 (1 df), p < ·001
Legitimate/illegitimate adopted.
  Chi-square (overall) = 18·59 (4 df), p < ·001
  Chi-square (trend) = 16·30 (1 df), p < ·001

TABLE A10.2: *Teacher's assessment of oral ability*

TEACHER'S ASSESSMENT	ILLEGITIMATE		LEGITIMATE
	Not Adopted	*Adopted*	
	%	%	%
Very good	6·9	14·4	11·2
Good	9·2	23·3	14·5
Average	51·9	48·0	52·9
Below average	25·5	13·0	17·5
Poor	6·6	1·4	3·8
Total tested	100·0 (349)	100·0 (146)	100·0 (14,524)

Legitimate/illegitimate not adopted.
  Chi-square (overall) = 31·57 (4 df), $p < ·001$
  Chi-square (trend) = 28·44 (1 df), $p < ·001$
Legitimate/illegitimate adopted.
  Chi-square (overall) = 13·57 (4 df), $p < ·01$
  Chi-square (trend) = 9·58 (1 df), $p < ·01$

TABLE A10.3: *Teacher's assessment of creativity*

TEACHER'S ASSESSMENT	ILLEGITIMATE		LEGITIMATE
	Not Adopted	*Adopted*	
Marked originality	2·9	3·4	2·7
Usually original	10·3	17·8	16·8
Some imagination	42·8	45·2	47·9
Little originality	38·5	30·8	29·4
No creativity	5·5	2·7	3·3
Total assessed	100·0 (348)	100·0 (146)	100·0 (14,510)

Legitimate/illegitimate not adopted.
  Chi-square (overall) = 24·64 (4 df), $p < ·001$
  Chi-square (trend) = 18·93 (1 df), $p < ·001$
Legitimate/illegitimate adopted.
  Chi-square (overall) = 0·84 (4 df), ns
  Chi-square (trend) = 0·10 (1 df), ns

TABLE A10.4: *Draw-a-man test*

SCORES	ILLEGITIMATE		LEGITIMATE
	Not Adopted	*Adopted*	
	%	%	%
0– 9	3·3	0·0	1·4 ⎱
10–19	37·2	26·5	26·7 ⎰ †
20–29	43·4	58·3	49·1
30–39	15·8	9·1	21·4 ⎱
40 +	0·0	6·1	1·4 ⎰ ‡
Total	100·0	100·0	100·0
tested	(336)	(132)	(14,195)

†Combined for illegitimate adopted chi-square test.
‡Combined for illegitimate not adopted chi-square test.
Legitimate/illegitimate not adopted.
   Chi-square (overall) = 29·73 (3 df), p < ·001
   Chi-square (trend) = 20·07 (1 df), p < ·001
Legitimate/illegitimate adopted.
   Chi-square (overall) = 32·28 (3 df), p < ·001
   Chi-square (trend) = 7·50 (1 df), p < ·01

TABLE A10.5: *Reading ability*

READING ABILITY	ILLEGITIMATE		LEGITIMATE
	Not Adopted	*Adopted*	
Poor	%	%	%
(0–20)	48·7	18·4	28·1
Average			
(21–28)	31·0	44·7	39·6
Good			
(29–30)	20·3	36·9	32·4
Total	100·0	100·0	100·0
tested	(345)	(151)	(14,387)

Legitimate/illegitimate not adopted.
   Chi-quare (overall) = 71·50 (2 df), p < ·001
   Chi-square (trend) = 59·35 (1 df), p < ·001
Legitimate/illegitimate adopted.
   Chi-square (overall) = 6·47 (2 df), p < ·05
   Chi-square (trend) = 4·67 (1 df), p < ·05

TABLE A10.7: *Arithmetical ability*

ARITHMETICAL ABILITY	ILLEGITIMATE		LEGITIMATE
	Not Adopted	*Adopted*	
	%	%	%
Poor (0–3)	38·3	31·4	28·2
Average (4–6)	40·9	37·9	41·0
Good (7–10)	20·9	30·7	30·8
Total tested	100·0 (345)	100·0 (140)	100·0 (14,418)

Legitimate/illegitimate not adopted.
  Chi-square (overall) = 22·95 (2 df), p < ·001
  Chi-square (trend) = 22·93 (1 df), p < ·001
Legitimate/illegitimate adopted.
  Chi-square (overall) = 0·85 (2 df), ns
  Chi-square (trend) = 0·26 (1 df), ns

ANALYSIS A10.6: *Analysis of Reading Score*

Main effects model.

Dependent variable is transformed Southgate Reading Test Score.

Independent variables are as shown below.

Sample size = 12202

Mean score = 1·144

Fitted Constants and Analysis of Variance table

x^2 values are adjusted for the other factors

Source		Fitted Constant	DF	x^2	
Overall		1·070			
Birthweight Coefficient: (increase per kg measured about 3·363 kg)		·051	1	116·52	***
Husband's 1965: Social Class	SCI + II + IIINM	·107	3	646·00	***
	SC IIIM	— ·008			
	SC IV + V	— ·065			
	No male head	— ·034			
Sex:	Girl	·046	1	322·20	***
	Boy	— ·046			
Age Coefficient: (increase per year measured about 7·0 years)		·132	1	64·28	***
Number of Children:	1–2	·050	2	369·27	***
	3	·015			
	4 +	— ·065			
Legitimate/ Illegitimate Groups	Illegitimate adopted	·048	2	38·65	***
	Illegitimate not adopted	— ·079			
	Legitimate	·031			

Residual mean square = ·0773

Total variance   = ·0884

ANALYSIS A10.8: *Analysis of Arithmetic Score*

Main effects model.

Dependent variable is transformed arithmetic score.

Independent variables are as shown below.

Sample size = 12224

Mean score = ·8055

Fitted Constants and Analysis of Variance table
x^2 values are adjusted for the other factors

Source		Fitted Constant	DF	x^2	
Overall		·739			
Birthweight Coefficient: (increase per kg measured about 3·363 kg)		·048	1	105·48	***
Husband's 1965: Social Class	SCI + II + III NM	·077	3	378·43	***
	SC IIIM	— ·015			
	SC IV + V	— ·050			
	No male head	— ·012			
Sex:	Girl	— ·007	1	7·81	**
	Boy	·007			
Age Coefficient: (increase per year measured about 7·0 years)		·173	1	123·34	***
Number of Children:	1–2	·019	2	45·23	***
	3	·002			
	4 +	— ·021			
Legitimate/ Illegitimate Groups	Illegitimate adopted	·001	2	21·11	***
	Illegitimate not adopted	— ·039			
	Legitimate	·038			

Residual mean square = ·0742
Total variance   = ·0789

TABLE A10.9: *Teacher's assessment of maternal interest*

MATERNAL INTEREST	ILLEGITIMATE		LEGITIMATE
	Not Adopted	*Adopted*	
	%	%	%
No interest	29·3	4·3	14·7
Some interest	40·5	27·7	39·5
Very interested	19·0	56·7	36·0
Over concerned	1·1	5·0	2·8
Don't know or inapplicable	10·1	6·4	7·1
Total with information	100·0	100·0	100·0
	(348)	(141)	(14,512)
No information	4·9	11·9	2·9
Grand total	100·0	100·0	100·0
	(366)	(160)	(14,949)

Legitimate/illegitimate not adopted (excluding DK or inapplicable).
   Chi-square (overall) = 81·17 (3 df), p < ·001
   Chi-square (trend) = 76·97 (1 df), p < ·001
Legitimate/illegitimate adopted (excluding DK or inapplicable).
   Chi-square (overall) = 30·76 (3 df), p < ·001
   Chi-square (trend) = 29·52 (1 df), p < ·001

TABLE A10.10: *Teacher's assessment of paternal interest*

| PATERNAL INTEREST | ILLEGITIMATE | | LEGITIMATE |
	Not Adopted	*Adopted*	
	%	%	%
No interest	23·6	8·6	15·4
Some interest	13·5	15·0	22·6
Very interested	8·1	40·7	24·9
Over concerned	0·0	2·9	1·7
Don't know or inapplicable	54·9	32·9	35·9
Total with information	100·0	100·0	100·0
	(348)	(140)	(14,477)
No information	4·9	12·5	3·2
Grand total	100·0	100·0	100·0
	(366)	(160)	(14,949)

Legitimate/illegitimate not adopted, by paternal interest (including DK category)[1].

Chi-square = 103·56 (3 df), p< ·001

Legitimate/illegitimate not adopted, by paternal interest (excluding DK category)[1].

Chi-square (overall) = 70·96 (2 df), p< ·001

Chi-square (trend) = 64·22 (1 df), p< ·001

Legitimate/illegitimate adopted, by paternal interest (including DK category).

Chi-square = 25·46 (4 df), p< ·001

Legitimate/illegitimate adopted, by paternal interest (excluding DK category).[1]

Chi-square (overall) = 22·85 (2 df), p< ·001

Chi-square (trend) = 19·04 (1 df), p< ·001

[1]Very interested and over-interested are combined.

ANALYSIS A11.1: *Analysis of Stott total score*

Main effects model.

Dependent variable is transformed Stott Total Score.

Independent variables are as shown below.

Sample size = 12181

Mean score = 2·677

Fitted Constants and Analysis of Variance table

x^2 values are adjusted for the other factors

Source		Fitted Constant	DF	x^2	
Overall		2·924			
Birthweight Coefficient: (increase per kg measured about 3·363 kg)		— ·165	1	50·66	***
Husband's 1965:	SCI + II + IIINM	— ·318	3	219·88	***
Social Class	SC IIIM	— ·027			
	SC IV + V	·174			
	No male head	·171			
Sex:	Girl	— ·243	1	389·13	***
	Boy	·243			
Number of Children:	1–2	— ·115	2	99·72	***
	3	— ·058			
	4 +	·173			
Legitimate/	Illegitimate adopted	— ·015	2	22·93	***
Illegitimate	Illegitimate not adopted	·206			
Groups	Legitimate	— ·191			

Residual mean square = 1·8105

Total variance = 1·9320

TABLE A11.2: *Summary of Maladaptive Behaviour Syndromes*

	ILLEGITIMATE	ADOPTED
1	Unforthcomingness	
2	Depression	—
3	Withdrawal	
4	Anxiety for Acceptance by Adults	—
5	*Hostility to Adults*†	*Hostility to Adults*
6	*Hostility to Children*	*Hostility to Children*
7	—	*Anxiety for acceptance by Children*
8	*Unconcern for adult approval*	
9	*Inconsequential behaviour*	*Inconsequential behaviour*
10	*Restlessness*	*Restlessness*§
11	*Miscellaneous*	
12‡	—	—

†Syndromes in italics remained significantly maladaptive after allowing for social class, sex and family size effects in an analysis of variance.

‡12th syndrome was 'Miscellaneous Nervous' shown by neither group.

§Significant only in analysis of variance.

REFERENCES

BAIRD, D. (1952). 'Preventive medicine in obstetrics', *New England J. Med.*, **246**, 561–8.

BARKER, D. J. P. and EDWARDS, J. H. (1967). 'Obstetric complications and school performance', *Brit. Med. J.*, **3**, 5567, 695–9.

BERNSTEIN, B. (1958). 'Some sociological determinants of perception (a theory of social learning)', *Brit. J. Sociol.*, **9**, 159–74.

BERNSTEIN, B. and SAUBER, M. (1960). *Deterrents to Early Pre-Natal Care, and Social Services Among Women Pregnant Out-of-Wedlock.* Albany, NY: NY State Dept. of Social Welfare.

BERNSTEIN, R. (1960). 'Are we still stereotyping the unmarried mother?' *Social Work*, **5**, 22–38.

BHAPKAR, V. P. (1968). 'On the analysis of contingency tables with a quantitative response', *Biometrics*, **24**, 329–38.

BOWLBY, J. (1951). *Maternal Care and Mental Health.* Monograph series of the World Health Organization, **2**.

BRAMALL, M. E. (1963). 'Unmarried parents—indications for social policy.' In: *New Thinking for Changing Needs.* Association of Social Workers, 16–28.

BRANSBY, E. R. and ELLIOTT, R. A. (1959). 'The unmarried mother and her child', *Monthly Bull. of Min. Health & Public Health Lab. Service*, **18**, 17–25.

BUTLER, N. R. and ALBERMAN, E. ed (1969). *Perinatal problems. Second Report of the 1958 British Perinatal Mortality Survey.* London: Livingstone.

BUTLER, N. R. and BONHAM, G. H. (1963). *Perinatal mortality. First Report of the 1958 British Perinatal Mortality Survey.* London: Livingstone.

CHAZAN, M. (1968). 'Recent research on maladjustment', *Brit. J. Educ. Psychol.*, **38**, 1, 5–7.

CHILD WELFARE LEAGUE OF AMERICA (1960). *Standards for Services to Unmarried Parents.* New York: Child Welfare League of America.

CHILD WELFARE LEAGUE OF AMERICA (1962). *Research Perspectives on the Unmarried Mother.* New York: Child Welfare League of America.

COMMITTEE ON LOCAL AUTHORITY AND ALLIED PERSONAL SERVICES (1968). *Report.* (Frederic Seebohm, Chairman). London: HM Stationery Office.

COMMITTEE ON HOUSING IN GREATER LONDON (1965). *Report of the Committee on Housing in Greater London, Chairman: Sir Milner Holland.* HM Stationery Office.

COOPER, C. (1955). 'The Illegitimate Child', *The Practitioner*, **174**, 1042, 488–93.

COSTIGAN, B. H. (1965). 'The unmarried mother: her decision regarding adoption', *Soc. Service Rev.*, **39**, 347.

DAVIE, R., BUTLER, N. R. and GOLDSTEIN, H. (1971). *From Birth to Seven.* London: Longman in association with the National Children's Bureau (in the press).

DEPARTMENTAL COMMITTEE ON THE ADOPTION OF CHILDREN (1970). *Adoption of Children.* (Working paper containing provisional proposals). London: HM Stationery Office

DEPARTMENT OF EDUCATION AND SCIENCE: CENTRAL ADVISORY COUNCIL FOR EDUCATION (ENGLAND) (1967). *Children and Their Primary Schools*. (The Plowden Report). London: HM Stationery Office.

DEPARTMENT OF EDUCATION AND SCIENCE (1969). *The Health of the school child: report of the Chief Medical Officer—for years 1966-68*. London: HM Stationery Office.

DEPARTMENT OF HEALTH, (1970). 'Confidential inquiry into post-neonatal deaths, 1964-66'. (By F. Riley). (*Reports on Public Health and Medical Subjects, No. 125*). London: HM Stationery Office.

DEWAR, D. (1968). *Orphans of the Living—a study of bastardy*. London: Hutchinson.

DINNAGE, R. (1970). *The Handicapped Child: Research Review, Vol. I*. London: Longman in association with the National Children's Bureau.

DINNAGE, R. and PRINGLE, M. L. KELLMER (1967a). *Residential Child Care—Facts and Fallacies*. London: Longman in association with the National Children's Bureau.

DINNAGE, R. and PRINGLE, M. L. KELLMER (1967b). *Foster Care—Facts and Fallacies*. London: Longman in association with the National Children's Bureau.

DOUGLAS, J. W. B. (1948). *Maternity in Great Britain*. London: Oxford University Press.

DOUGLAS, J. W. B. (1960). 'Premature children at primary school', *Brit. Med. J.*, **1**, 1008.

DOUGLAS, J. W. B. (1964). *The Home and the School*. London: MacGibbon & Kee.

DOUGLAS, J. W. B. and BLOMFIELD, J. M. (1958). *Children Under Five*. London: Allen & Unwin.

DRILLIEN, C. M. (1964). *The Growth and Development of the Prematurely Born Infant*. London: Livingstone.

DRILLIEN, C. M. (1965). 'The effect of obstetrical hazard on the later development of the child, and school disposal and performance for children of different birthweight born 1953-6', *Archives of Child Health*, **44**, 562-9.

EDWARDS, M. E. (1954). 'Failure and success in the adoption of toddlers', *Case Conference*, **1**, 3-8.

EDWARDS, H. and THOMPSON, B. (1970). 'Who are the fatherless?' *New Soc.* Feb. 4th, No. **436**, 192-3.

FELDSTEIN, M. S. and BUTLER, N. R. (1965). 'Analysis of factors affecting perinatal mortality. A multivariate statistical approach', *Brit. J. Prev. & Soc. Med.*, **19**, 128-34.

GARMEZY, E. (1968). 'Meeting the problems of illegitimacy the Danish way'. In: *Effective Services for Unmarried Parents and their Children: Innovative Community Approaches*. New York: National Council for Illegitimacy.

GENERAL REGISTER OFFICE (1964). *Statistical Review of England and Wales*. London: HM Stationery Office.

GENERAL REGISTER OFFICE (1966). *Classification of Occupations*. London: HM Stationery Office.

GENERAL REGISTER OFFICE (1967). *Statistical Review of England and Wales, Part 3, 1964*. London: HM Stationery Office.

GENERAL REGISTER OFFICE (1968). *Statistical Review of England and Wales, Part 3, 1965. Generation Study of Illegitimate Children*. London: HM Stationery Office, 74-86.

GILL, D., KOPLIK, L. H. and ILLSLEY, R. (1968). 'Pregnancy in Teenage Girls, I and II', (Mimeograph).

GIOVANNONI, J. M. (1970). 'Ethnic variation in the care and protection of children of single parents'. In: *Illegitimacy: Changing Services for Changing Times*. New York: Nat. Council on Illegitimacy, 86–98.

GRAY, P. G. and PARR, E. A. (1957). *Children in Care, and Recruitment of Foster Parents*. Social Survey.

GREVE, J., PAGE, D. and GREVE, S. (1971). *Homelessness in London*. Centre of Urban and Regional Studies, Univ. of Birmingham.

HAMMOND, W. H., STEEL, F. M. and ELLIOTT, R. (1960). 'A final study of unmarried mothers and their children', *Moral Welfare*, July, 79–87.

HARPER, P. A. and WIENER, G. (1965). 'Sequelae of low birthweight', *Annual Rev. Med.*, **16**, 405–20.

HARRIS, D. B. (1963). *Children's Drawings as Measures of Intellectual Maturity*. New York: Harcourt, Brace & World.

HERZOG, E. and SUDIA, C. (1968). 'Fatherless Homes: a Review of Research', *Children*, **15**, 5, 177–82.

HUMPHREY, M. (1969). *The Hostage Seekers*. London: Longman in association with the National Children's Bureau.

HOLMAN, R. (1970). *Unsupported Mothers*. Mothers in Action.

ILLSLEY, R. (1967). 'The sociological study of reproduction and its outcome'. In: RICHARDSON, S. A. and GUTTMACHER, A. F., *Child Bearing, its Social and Physical Aspects*. London: Williams and Wilkins, 73–141.

ILLSLEY, R. and GILL, D. (1968). 'Changing trends in illegitimacy's *Soc. Sci. & Med.*, **2**, 4, 415–33.

JOY, C. and STEEL, E. M. (1957). 'What happens afterwards: a survey of unmarried mothers and their children after 3 years, 1952–55', *Moral Welfare*, January, 12–17.

KAHN, J. H. and NURSTEN, J. P. (1968, 2nd ed.). *Unwillingly to School*. London: Pergamon.

LEES, J. P. and STEWART, A. H. (1957). 'Family or sibship position and scholastic ability', *Sociological Rev.*, **5**, 85–106.

LEISSNER, A. (1967). *Family Advice Services*. London: Longman in association with the National Children's Bureau.

LEISSNER, A., HERDMAN, A. and DAVIES, E. (1971). *Advice, Guidance and Assistance*. London: Longman in association with the National Children's Bureau.

LEVY, D. (1955). 'A follow-up study of unmarried mothers', *Soc. Casework*, **36**, 27–33.

LIPWORTH, L. and SPICER, C. (1966). *Regional and Social Factors in Infant Mortality*. General Register Office. London: HM Stationery Office.

McDONALD, A. (1967). *Children of Very Low Birthweight*. London: Heinemann in conjunction with Spastics Society Medical, Education and Information Unit.

McDONALD, E. K. (1956). 'Follow-up of illegitimate children', *The Medical Officer*, **96**, 361–5.

MAPSTONE, E. (1969). 'Children in care', *Concern*, **3**, National Children's Bureau, London, 23–8.

MARSDEN, D. (1969). *Mothers Alone*. Harmondsworth: Allen Lane, The Penguin Press.

MEYER, H. J., BORGATTA, E. F. and FANSHIEL, D. (1959). 'Unwed mothers' decisions about their babies', *Child Welfare*, **38**, 1–6.

MILLER, F. J. W., *et al.* (1960). *Growing-up in Newcastle upon Tyne*. London: Oxford University Press.

MONCRIEFF, SIR ALAN, (1961). Standing Conference of Societies registered for Adoption, Conference Report, 5.

MORRIS, F. S. (1956). 'What happens to illegitimate babies', *Child Care*, **10**, 4–9.

NATIONAL CHILDREN'S BUREAU, (1971). 'A national study of one-parent families' *Concern*, 7.

NATIONAL COUNCIL FOR THE UNMARRIED MOTHER AND HER CHILD (1968). *The Human Rights of Those Born Out of Wedlock*.

NATIONAL COUNCIL FOR THE UNMARRIED MOTHER AND HER CHILD (1971). *Evidence to the Committee on one-parent families*. Unpublished Memorandum.

NICHOLSON, J. (1968). *Mother and Baby Homes*. London: Allen & Unwin.

NISSEL, M. ed. (1970). *Social Trends*. Central Stastical Office. London: HM Stationery Office.

PACKMAN, J. (1968). *Child Care: Needs and Numbers*. London: Allen & Unwin.

PAKTER, J., *et al*. (1961). 'Out of wedlock births in New York city I: Sociological aspects II: Medical aspects', *Amer. J. Pub. Health*, **51**, 5, 683–96; **6**, 846–65.

POCHIN, J. (1969). *Without a Wedding Ring*. London: Constable.

POND, D. A. and ARIE, T. (1971). 'Services for children in trouble', *Child Care*, **25**, 1, 16–20.

PRINGLE, M. L. KELLMER (1971, 2nd ed.). *Deprivation and Education*. London: Longman in association with the National Children's Bureau.

PRINGLE, M. L. KELLMER ed. (1965). *Investment in Children*. London: Longman.

PRINGLE, M. L. KELLMER (1966). *Adoption—Facts and Fallacies*. London: Longman in association with the National Children's Bureau.

PRINGLE, M. L. KELLMER ed. (1969). *Caring for Children*. London: Longman in association with the National Children's Bureau.

PRINGLE, M. L. KELLMER, BUTLER, N. R. and DAVIE, R. (1966). 11,000 *Seven-year-olds*. London: Longman.

PRINGLE, M. L. KELLMER and PICKUP, K. T. (1963). 'The reliability and validity of the Goodenough Draw-a-man Test', *Brit. J. Educ. Psychol.*, **33**, 3, 297–306.

RAWLINGS, G., REYNOLDS, E. O. R., STEWART, A. and STRANG, L. B. (1971). 'Changing prognosis for infants of very low birthweight', *The Lancet*, **1**, 7698, 516–19.

RECORD, R. G., McKEOWN, T. and EDWARDS, J. H. (1969). 'Relation of measure of intelligence to birthweight and duration of gestation.' *Annals of Human Genetics*, **33**, 71–9.

REED, E. F. and LATIMER, R. (1963). *A Study of Unmarried Mothers who Kept Their Babies*. Cincinatti: Social Welfare Research Inc.

RICHARDSON, I. (1967). Perspective for tomorrow. In: *Welfare State and Welfare Society* (National Council of Social Service).

ROBERTS, R. W. (1966). *The Unwed Mother*. New York: Harper & Rowe.

RODMAN, H. (1963). 'The lower class value stretch', *Social Forces*, **42**, 205–15.

RODMAN, H. (1966). 'Illegitimacy in the Caribbean social structure: a reconsideration', *Amer. Sociol. Rev.*, **31**, 5, 673–83.

ROME, R. (1939). 'A study of some factors entering into unmarried mothers' decision regarding the disposition of her child'. Unpublished Thesis. New York: Smith College School for Welfare Work.

ROYAL COMMISSION ON THE STATUS OF WOMEN IN CANADA, (1970). A Report. Information Canada.

RUDERMAN, F. A. (1968). *Child Care and Working Mothers*. Child Welfare League of America.

SAUBER, M. (1970). 'Life situations of mothers whose first child was born out of wedlock: a follow-up after six years'. In: *Illegitimacy; Changing Services for Changing Times*, National Council on Illegitimacy, New York, 40–53.

SAUBER, M. and CORRIGAN, E. M. (1970). *The Six-Year Experience of Unwed Mothers as Parents*. Community Council of Greater New York.

SAUBER, M. and RUBINSTEIN, E. (1965). *Experiences of the Unwed Mother as a Parent; a Longitudinal Study of Unmarried Mothers Who Keep Their First-Born*. New York: Community Council of Greater New York.

SCHOFIELD, M. (1965). *The Sexual Behaviour of Young People*. London: Longman, Greens.

SCOTTISH COUNCIL FOR THE UNMARRIED MOTHER AND HER CHILD. (1967). *Unmarried Mothers, Their Medical and Social Needs*. Report of a day conference. Standing Conference of Societies Registered for Adoption.

SHAPIRO, P. C. (1968). Illegitimacy and Child Care. *New Society*, **277**, 18th January, 87–88.

SOUTHGATE, V. (1962). *Southgate Group Reading Tests. Manual of Instructions*. University of London Press.

SPENCE, J. C. *et al.*, (1954). *A Thousand Families in Newcastle upon Tyne*. Oxford University Press.

STEEL, E. M. (1957). 'Further surveys of unmarried mothers and their children', *Moral Welfare*, March, 50–54.

STOLTZ, L. M. (1960). 'Effects of maternal employment on children', *Child Development*, **31**, 749–82.

STOTT, D. H. (1966, 3rd ed.). *The Social adjustment of children—manual to the Bristol Social Adjustment Guides*. University of London Press.

TANNER, J. M. (1960). *Human Growth*. London: Pergamon.

THOMPSON, B. (1956). 'A social study of illegitimate maternities'. *Brit. J. Prev. & Soc. Med.* **10**, 2, 75–87.

THE TIMES (1971). The responsible family. *First Leader*, 16th June.

TORONTO AND DISTRICT WELFARE COUNCIL. (unmarried Parenthood Sub-Committee), (1943). *A Study of the Adjustment of Teenage Children Born out of Wedlock who Remained in the Custody of their Mothers or Relatives*. Welfare Council of Toronto and District.

TYERMAN, M. J. (1968). *Truancy*. University of London Press.

VINCENT, C. E. (1961). *Unmarried Mothers*. New York: Free Press.

WEIR, S. (1970). *A study of unmarried mothers and their children in Scotland*. Scottish Health Service Studies, No. 13. Scottish Home and Health Department.

WIENER, G., RIDER, R. V., OPPEL, W. C., FISCHER, L. K. and HARPER, P. A. (1965). 'Correlates of low birthweight: physchological status at six and seven years of age', *Paediatrics*, **35**, 434–44.

WIMPERIS, V. (1960). *The Unmarried Mother and her Child*. London: Allen & Unwin.

WISEMAN, S. (1970). 'The educational obstacle race.' Director's address to the Annual Conference. Slough: NFER.

WRIGHT, H. (1965). 80 *Unmarried Mothers Who Kept Their Babies*. Sacramento: State of California Department of Social Welfare.

WYNN, M. (1964). *Fatherless Families*. London: Michael Joseph.

YARROW, A. (1964). 'Illegitimacy in South-East Essex', *Medical Officer*, **111**, 24th January, 47–8.

YELLOLY, M. A. (1964). 'Social casework with unmarried parents: a critical evaluation of its theoretical aspects in the light of a study of extra-marital pregnancies'. Unpublished PhD Thesis, University of Liverpool.

YELLOLY, M. A. (1965). 'Factors relating to an adoption decision by the mothers of illegitimate infants', *Soc. Rev.*, **13**, 6–13.

YOUNG, L. (1954). *Out of Wedlock*. London: McGraw-Hill.

YOUNG, M. and MCGEENEY, P. (1968). *Learning begins at home*. London: Routledge & Kegan Paul.

YOUNGHUSBAND, E., BIRCHALL, D., DAVIE, R. and PRINGLE, M. L. KELLMER (1970). *Living with Handicap*. National Children's Bureau.

YUDKIN, S. and HOLME, A. (1963). *Working Mothers and Their Children*. London: Michael Joseph.

YUDKIN, S. (1967). 0–5; *A Report on the Care of Pre-school Children*. National, Society of Children's Nurseries, London.

Cobalt *ii*

Al-Ţag *et al* (1984) fuller *et al* (199?) argue *et al*. Abbasi *el al.*
study of the relation in the effect of high acidity in solution and of its
presence. Unpublished PhD Thesis, University, Nottingham.

Hassan, Ab Alalla, studying the soil composition. Unpublished PhD
of the compound *et al*. Academic Press, New York.

Waugh, A (1965) family display. London, Macmillan.

Williams *et al* (1986). Critical fundamentals on selection in the
Symphylella. New Delhi.

Wolff Hanson, A., Bradley, E., Elliott, A. and composite, M. (1989)
A 17 fixation cycle sterile. Journal of Endocrinology, London.

Wright, S and Frost, L. in the consideration of the Cambridge Congress
23. end London.

Yamouti *et al*, the effect of compositions of the soil in mineral soils.
gcase of Chemistry, Imperial, London.